SCHOOL VIOLENCE

SCHOOL VIOLENCE
Studies in Alienation, Revenge, and Redemption

Ingrid Rose

KARNAC

First published in 2009 by
Karnac Books Ltd
118 Finchley Road
London NW3 5HT

British Library Cataloguing in Publication Data

A C.I.P. for this book is available from the British Library

ISBN-13: 978-1-85575-613-7

Typeset by Vikatan Publishing Solutions (p) Ltd., Chennai, India

Printed in Great Britain

www.karnacbooks.com

CONTENTS

ACKNOWLEDGEMENTS

I wish to acknowledge, with heartfelt gratitude, the many children and adolescents with whom I have worked over the years. I have been a witness to their struggles and triumphs. My special appreciation goes to the youth who have suffered through the indignities of being teased, excluded, expelled, and in the worst cases, imprisoned. Thank you for keeping the spirit of hope alive.

To my own children, Sean, Dana, Darryl, and Rowan.
You have been my greatest teachers. May your paths through life bring joy and fulfillment.

PREFACE

"Yes! Violence at school is a topic, which has to be taken seriously! That is why I want everyone to know: I am against it!" a member of a panel which I attended exclaimed loud and clear. The audience applauded and confirmed his stance: a courageous man they thought! The panel was assembled in order to debate the causes of school violence and propose possible remedies. Judging from the atmosphere in the hall it seemed clear: Bullying, teasing, blackmail, fist fights or shootings ought to be condemned and perpetuators strictly punished. We all have to give our best, in order to protect students from violent acts or ruthless bullying! Methods were suggested: zero tolerance, metal detectors, video cameras, more policing and of course the implementation of rigorous behaviour codes in schools. The general consensus was that violence at school can only be abated when we tackle the roots: No brawls on the playground, no teasing of the awkward students or drawings of violence.

This approach to violence is widespread. Politicians, school administrators and even psychologists believe, that drawing the line is the *only* acceptable answer to violence. The seriousness of the issue forces us to implement hard measures. Psycho-talk or lengthy speculations about causes are considered gibberish or a sign of leniency.

Violence at schools calls for *doers*, who can execute concrete, definite programs. We need to eradicate the causes of violence at school. School violence is considered *atrocious* and *vile*. To oppose violence is considered a moral duty. The result: Punishments and behaviour modification programs are introduced in order to render the students peaceful and fight the evilness of violence in the core. A myriad of programs are offered, which claim to help schools to eliminate violence. Training programs for soft skills, emotional intelligence or empathy form part of many schools curricula. Students are taught conflict management and anger control. Brawls, teasing, cell-phones and or ego-shooters are banned from schools, because they are perceived as possible causes of violence.

Naturally, no sane person endorses or promotes violence at school. We all want our schools to be institutions where children thrive and develop into healthy, responsible and peaceful beings. Schools should be a safe heaven for children and adolescents. Violence has to be banned. So what is wrong with condemning school violence and calling for strict measures?

There are several snags in this very common approach. When an issue is tagged as abominable, discussed in the media and among experts, then the danger lurks, that *we stop thinking*. We might suspect the usual culprits and propose the same solutions. Instead of brooding over possible answers and the background of the problem, we rehearse ourselves as vigilantes. Because the topic shocks us, we start to look for *quick fixes* and fail to look the problem in the eye. In other words: we fall into the *morality trap*. We rebuke violence without realizing that we cannot get rid of violence by moral exclamations alone. Morality can even be part of a defence system to impede unwanted insights or disturbing conclusions. By quoting moral categories and demanding concrete answers we might even *distance* ourselves from the actual issue. In order to stay clean, we devalue an event or phenomenon.

Schools are prone to fall into that trap. The pedagogical eye sees violence as bad, an irritation and not an opportunity to learn something about the emotions and fantasies of students. This attitude is understandable: The duty of schools is to teach students life skills. They provide children with *answers* and help them to distinguish between right and wrong. *Knowing* is important, confusions should be avoided. Disturbances aggravate the educational ritual. Teachers can then no longer fulfil their role as master of ceremony, instructing the younger generation on what to do and framing their realities. As schools belong the realm of Apollo, violence is a clear *antidote* to what schools are about. Conflicts breaks things up and release hidden forces. The danger is, that the system cannot function according to their rules and regulations. The demons are let loose and irritate the system. This is one reason why educationalists are often reluctant to contemplate the in depth meaning of violence.

Fact is though, that violence *belongs* to human nature. Violence is not just an aberration, the result of misunderstandings or bad influence: it is embedded in our souls. Easy remedies and quick fixes often remain on the surface. They deal with the symptoms, without investigating the deeper, psychological causes. When someone commits a violent act, then he might not just be a fellow being led astray, but someone struggling with *inner forces*. His or her violence contains a message. Ferocious plots or ruthless fights often fascinate students. This attraction to violence might be an attempt to connect with another realm of psyche, come into contact with unconscious topics. Maybe the students are trying to connect to their shadow and are hoping to develop imagery for their inappropriate need. When students start bullying each other, engage in fights or are fascinated by weapons, then maybe they are challenging their shadow. For everyone who deals with students it should be paramount that we should not just condemn violence, but look into the subjective realities of the people involved. Their fantasies and stories might tell us something that is important.

Schools have another problem. In our society children still carry a lot of *projections*. Often they are even considered as beings, which are beyond evil. Their aggressions are therefore not seen as the result of their endeavours, but excused by the surroundings, computer-games, the media or peer-influence. Violent children are believed to be victims of childhood trauma, a toxic family situation or societal tensions. We fail to respect their desire to be bad. This image is problematic. Children also have a shadow, struggle with abysmal fantasies or aggressive drives. They are not per se better human beings, but share the same psychic structure as grown ups. When we perceive children only as victims, we might fail to respect their psychology. We leave them alone in their struggle to come to terms with their shadow.

This book offers an alternative. It dares to include the subjective realities of students and teachers. It avoids moralizations and simple answers, but looks at violence form the in- and outside. It tackles the important problem that repression of violence can lead to an increased fascination. Rose not only offers a lot of new insights, she also presents a lot of valuable, experienced methods on how we should deal with violence at school. The book can be highly recommended and should be read by anyone who deals with conflict at schools or wants to understand the psychological situation of children in the school system.

Allan Guggenbühl

ABSTRACT

School violence

Studies in alienation, revenge, and redemption

Ingrid Rose

Summary

Experiences of violence in schools are encountered much more frequently than they used to be. The shocking repercussions of these
acts are felt nation-wide and particularly impact school populations,
families, and communities. This book undertakes to illuminate factors pertaining to the phenomenon of school violence.

The effects of historical and current issues impacting the school
system are linked to the development of intrapsychic phenomena
influencing aggressive expression and behavioural reactions of
school students. Individual, social, and cultural phenomena are
generally approached in a fashion that relies on views and interpretations agreed on by consensus of the mainstream population.
As a result layers of the psyche that lie closer to unconscious material, are often missed or disregarded. A method of exploration based
on depth psychology offers insight into lesser-known aspects of
awareness underlying more obvious behavioural dynamics. In this
way, greater understanding on both cognitive and experiential levels can be reached. Previously misunderstood or unacknowledged

qualities and processes, important to the individual and culture, can be illuminated. Practical ways of dealing with school problems can be offered both for individuals and for the system as a whole.

A Jungian lens is used to study how repression of aggression and violence on cultural and socio-political levels may lead to aggression. When there is no opportunity to express emotions made taboo in the system, the build up of disavowed material eventually manifests in impulsive behaviour, often with disastrous results. The perpetrator of aggression is little understood and often scapegoated or expelled from the school community. However, when individual and collective shadow material is acknowledged and unravelled, incidents of school aggression can be made meaningful for the whole school community.

Imaginal ideas and methods are introduced through the use of image, myth, and fairy tales. Process-oriented approaches show how awareness of body experiences and form give rise to images useful in understanding experiences underlying withdrawal or aggression. Composite case studies of work with individuals and in groups are introduced to illustrate the use of various techniques such as active imagination and dream exploration in addressing disturbing behaviour.

In exploring anti-social tendencies, deprivation and achievement-based standards in the school system are seen to be factors linked to individual experiences of shame, revenge, hatred, and anger. In attempting to fulfil needs for recognition and inclusion, aggressive acts may be a cry of hope that the individual's longing for attention will be filled. Acts of violence temporarily bring the individual a sense of power and provide connection with others, breaking through the wall of isolation in which the school disturber feels trapped. Psychodynamic issues such as grandiosity and power are introduced as they relate to expressions of violence. Group dialogue is explored as a means of de-escalating potentially violent situations, providing a safe space in which unexpressed attitudes and feelings can be released.

The theoretical and practical ideas offered in this book are illustrated through the introduction of composite case material and its analysis. Case examples of withdrawal, fighting, murderous impulses, school bullying, and shootings, are used to highlight ways of addressing presenting problems.

Importance, relevance, and aims

This book is intended for professionals such as school principals, teachers, social workers, psychologists, school administrators, school counsellors and all who work directly with youth in various contexts. It is also intended for parents, family and community members, youth advisors and mentors, youth group leaders, religious advisors, camp counsellors, and others interested in the well-being of children and adolescents.

Due to the increased incidence of school shootings and reports of school bullying it becomes apparent that this book is both timely and very needed. After the latest reports on the horrendous killings at Virginia Tech, the school shooting in Sweden, as well as the increasing numbers of school shootings over the last decade, there are many unanswered questions to what factors contribute to events of this sort. These questions are now in the forefront of the minds of many members of our society, particularly stirred up by the wide media coverage of the latest shootings. The insights that this book provides into occurrences of this sort are sorely needed and sought for, both nationally in the United States and in other places of the world.

What makes this book particularly interesting is its depth-oriented view into behavioural and systemic dynamics, rarely explored before in this context. Although there has been research conducted on the topic of school violence, this has mainly focused on a preventive approach, exploring factors that would curtail aggression in schools. Some of these methods include the use of metal detectors, the taboo of verbal and physical aggressive expression, the introduction of mediation training, and increased restrictions on children who act out. Underlying psychological factors, although sometimes mentioned within the framework of psychiatric medication models, have not been explored in a way that leads to enhanced understanding of what children and adolescents experience internally. Understanding their mindset has not been a major focus in available literature on the topic of school violence.

In exploring the inner worlds of disturbed students the aim of this book is twofold. One important aspect is to bring enhanced understanding of dynamics involved in incidents of school violence to professionals, family members, school staff, and the larger social system. In this way, I hope to awaken in each of us the awareness that the individual student is a person in his or her own right, with his or her own experiences, reactions, beliefs, and attitudes, with the right to be acknowledged and appreciated for those. In addressing the expectations of the school system and students' reactions to these, I hope to highlight that school disturbers are a reflection of a system that has its own symptoms needing to be addressed. The other facet of this book focuses on the introduction of tools and techniques that can be used to encourage out the inner experiences of students that usually remain unspoken and unaddressed. In utilizing dream figures, myth, image, body awareness, and group dialogue, previously ignored or repressed phenomena can find a place in which they can be contained and acknowledged. The aim here is to provide a toolkit offering a variety of techniques to both prevent and intervene in potential or actual episodes of escalating or violent behavior.

CHAPTER ONE

Setting the stage

Incidence of violence in schools

During 1996–97 approximately 4,000 incidents of rape or other types of sexual battery were reported in United States public schools. Weapons were used in about 11,000 incidents of physical attacks or fights and 7,000 robberies occurred in schools that year. Approximately 190,000 fights or physical attacks not involving weapons also occurred at schools in 1996–97, along with about 115,000 thefts and 98,000 incidents of vandalism (National Center for Education Statistics, 1997). In a survey conducted by the National Council for Education Statistics (NCES) in 2000 the following information was noted (National Center for Education Statistics, 2000). According to school principals, 71% of public elementary and secondary schools experienced at least one violent incident during the 1999–2000 school year (including rape, sexual battery other than rape, physical attacks or fights with and without a weapon, threats of physical attack with and without a weapon, and robbery with and without a weapon). In all, approximately 1,466,000 such incidents were reported in public schools in 1999–2000. One or more serious violent incidents (including rape, sexual battery other than rape, physical attacks or fights with a weapon, threats of physical attack with a weapon, and robbery with and without a weapon) occurred in 20 percent of public schools.

Controlling for all other factors, five school characteristics were related to the likelihood that a school would experience at least one serious violent incident: enrolment size, urbanicity, percentage of males, number of serious discipline problems, and number of school-wide disruptions. In the 1999–2000 school year, 20% of North American public schools experienced at least one serious violent incident. In those schools, about 61,700 serious violent incidents occurred. The most commonly occurring serious violent crime was the threat of attack with a weapon, with 11 percent of schools experiencing at least one such offence during that school year (National Center for Education Statistics, 2000).

School shootings

In 2001, the United States Congress requested that the National Research Council study the phenomenon of school violence that had been occurring in increasing frequency between the years of 1992 and 2001 (Moore, Petrie, Braga & McLaughlin, 2003). This report focused on specific incidents that included school shootings in which one or more students or teachers had been wounded or killed. Detailed case studies were developed on the perpetrator, the school situation, the community in which the violence took place, and the circumstances leading to the expression of violence. The committee failed to reach firm scientific conclusions about the causes of the shootings or suggest effective means of preventing or controlling them. However, the information gathered provides interesting insights into the psychological, emotional, and social dynamics present in the lives of both the shooters and the communities in which they lived. The data highlight areas such as experiences of alienation, teasing/bullying in schools, relationships within the school system between teachers and students and among students, shooter traits, and other factors.

In all cases studied it was found that youth perpetrators experienced alienation from adults in their communities and that parents had little information about what their children were really experiencing (Moore et al. 2003). A disconnection was detected between how adults and parents experienced the adolescent and the actual internal experiences of the adolescent. In addition, the evidence showed a separation between teachers and students relationally including little personal knowledge of students on the part of teachers. Parents and most teachers evidenced poor understanding of the children's exposure to changing community conditions, their experiences in social situations, and their interpretations of those experiences.

Most of the adolescent shooters had not been considered at high risk for violent behaviour. Although some of the student perpetrators were perceived as having a place in one or more groups within the school social scene, they were generally viewed as being on the margins of these groups. They saw themselves as being either "loners" or not quite belonging or fitting in anywhere within the social fabric. Shooters showed an intense concern about their social standing in their school and among their peers. Most had experienced recent changes in peer relations with attempts to affiliate with other "loners," kids with behaviour problems or fringe identities. In many cases, increased social withdrawal was noticed, with fearful, angry, or depressed mood becoming more evident. There was a common factor among the shooters of school grades falling in months prior to the attack and a resultant change in school status. In nearly all of the cases studied, the shooters had been victims of bullying by others. Another common element found was the presence of exclusivity in either mainstream or marginal student groups or cliques.

Adolescent mass murderers and school avengers were found to have the following characteristics. All were male, 80% were white, 70% were described as loners, 43% had been bullied by others, 37% came from divorced or separated families, 44% were described as "fantasizers", 42% had a history of violence of some sort, 46% had an arrest history, 62% had a substance abuse history, 48% were preoccupied with war or weapons, and 23% had a documented psychiatric history (Meloy, Hempel, Mohandie, Shiva & Gray 2001, p. 723). Classroom avengers were often found to be the victims of bullying and to be preoccupied with fantasies of murder. Classroom avengers were described as being likely to think about mass murder and to come up with a conscious plan. Studies also showed that school shootings are calculating and premeditated, motivated by vengeance (McGee & DeBernardo, 1999). Twelve shooting incidents in North American middle and high schools were examined between 1993 and 1998. The shooters were described as fantasizing about revenge and triumph over their adversaries, with vivid mental rehearsals of their chosen methods of violence. Guns, violent media, and bomb making had become special fascinations for them. The characteristics of these school avengers suggested a clinical diagnosis of atypical depression and mixed personality disorder with paranoid, antisocial, and narcissistic features. The typical profile of the school avenger based on the study of these 12 shooting incidents is described as follows:

> "A white male from a working or middle-class background living in a rural area or small city. Dysfunctional family background and relationships are likely. Parental discipline is often harsh or inconsistent. Problems with bonding and social attachments are common. Most likely depression manifests through sullen, angry, and irritable moods or actions. Blame for personal failure is easily projected on others. There is low tolerance for adversity with unstable self-esteem ranging from self-reproach to grandiosity" (McGee and DeBernardo 1999, p. 17).

Shooters often had a desperate need to let others know what they were planning and expressed it in journal entries, letters to others, threats, or boasts to peers.

Bullying

It was not until fairly recently (early 1970s) that bully/victim problems began to be studied systematically, initially in Scandinavia. Attempts to understand this phenomenon have been made in other countries since the late eighties, including the United States, Australia, and The Netherlands. Bullying or victimization is described as a student being bullied or victimized when he or she is exposed, repeatedly and over time, to negative actions on the part of one or more other students (Olweus 1993, p. 9).

Males tend to bully and be bullied more frequently than females. For males, physical and verbal bullying is most common; for females, verbal bullying (both taunting and insults of a sexual nature), and spreading rumours are more common. Bullying generally begins in the elementary grades, peaks in the sixth through the eighth grades and persists into high school. Bullying among primary age children has become recognized as an antecedent to more violent behaviour in later years. In addition, a negative school climate where negative behaviour gets most of the attention encourages the formation of cliques and bullying (Garrett 2003, p. 11). One of four children who bully will have a criminal record by the age of thirty. Factors considered as contributing to bullying and aggression are individual characteristics of the child, family atmosphere, peer influences, and school climate.

Through the use of extensive interviews with high school students and school personnel to highlight the degree to which bullying, harassment, stalking, intimidation, humiliation, and fear contribute to toxicity in the school environment, the following comes to light (Garbarino & deLara, 2002). Students' reports indicate the high numbers of youth who are traumatized on a daily basis in a variety of ways in classrooms, bathrooms, locker rooms, corridors, playgrounds, and buses, in situations that constellate intense fears of being unsafe for those students being preyed upon, as well as for those observing these acts of emotional violence. The effects of this kind of emotional violence are found to be just as traumatic as physical and sexual violence. The emotional wellbeing of these children suffers, often resulting in intense shame, depression, hopelessness, anger with a sense of helplessness, and sometimes the perpetration of bullying in return. In the worst cases, 'suicidality' or thoughts of attempting to harm or kill others emerge. The perpetrators of the Columbine High School shooting, Eric Harris and Dylan Klebold, were known to have been harassed, bullied, and put down on a daily basis for years (Garrett, 2003).

Another interesting fact evidenced in the interviews is how little trust these adolescents have in the ability or willingness of adults to do anything about the bullying situations. Teachers generally want to stay aloof from behaviours of this kind, believing it is not their domain to have to deal with student conflicts. Roughly 40% of bullied students in the primary grades and almost 60% in secondary/junior high reported that teachers try to put a stop to it only once in a while or almost never (Olweus, 1993). Only limited contact is made by teachers with the students involved in order to talk about the problems, particularly in junior high school. Sufficient adult involvement is shown to reduce the amount of bullying incidents.

However, parents of bullied students, and of those who bully, are often unaware of the problem or the extent of the problem. There is therefore little awareness of the necessity of talking with their children about difficulties. Parents who do have some knowledge of the bullying situation generally feel unable to intercede on behalf of students with the school authorities, or on the other hand, are either not interested in their children's problems, or suggest that their kids in turn beat up those inflicting the teasing or bullying. Those parents who do in fact take steps to address the difficulties are far in the minority. Some adolescents are afraid that if their parents do address this with school personnel, identifying the culprits, with no steps then being taken to rectify the situation, the ensuing consequences would be far worse for them.

Although many adults working in schools consider bullying to be a normal part of growing up, a rite of passage or part of a developmental stage, more and more states in the U.S. are beginning to require schools to adopt anti-bullying policies although, to date, not much has been done in terms of prevention (Limber & Small, 2003). Although many of the policies suggest complete weapon control, metal detectors, zero tolerance for bullying with severe consequences (Columbine High School, for instance, now has a zero tolerance for violence policy), (Columbine High School Massacre, 2006), school systems still do not provide a means for addressing the underlying problems of the individual and of the school culture. In the many interventions that are suggested for addressing bullying, little focus has been placed on how to address the actual bully or instigator. Mostly instigators are approached in a punitive, marginalizing, and shaming way, thus perpetuating and exacerbating the problem.

Education and the school system

Since the 1950s, American education in high schools has been dramatically influenced by the vision of educational administrator James Conant (Conant, 1959). In accord with Conant's attempts to universalize the high school system as an American institution, providing a milieu in which youth from a diverse range of social classes and groups could be brought together to receive a comprehensive education, by the 1960s high school had become more popular, reaching a wider range of North American youth. One of the effects of this was that adolescents became segregated from the rest of society for a significant amount of time each week, contributing to the development of a strong youth culture (Rury, 2005). As youth began to feel more identified with each other as a separate cultural component, the distance between other segments of the population increased. Youth culture has not only divorced youth from the larger community and acted as a point of departure from shared values, it has resulted in a set of youth subcultures, each a peer-based school society with its own distinct culture, set of values, and style. This dynamic has been described as a "peculiar contest of competing or co-existing groups, each pursuing its own goals" (p. 57), often with boundaries relatively closed to members of others groups who are often derogatized, stereotyped, or scapegoated. It is these dynamics that often contribute to experiences of bullying, teasing, and marginalization experienced by individual students seen as "loners" or on the fringes of cliques or culturally distinct subcultures. As the growth in size of schools increased dramatically, a greater number of students were found to be excluded from school activities, contributing to more widespread alienation from the institution. It appears that greater school size also inhibited student learning due to greater difficulty in meaningful communication and making personal contact (Haller, 1992). The increased size of schools made it difficult for students to identify with school as a community-oriented institution with a resultant level of disengagement and resistance. Schools had become referenced with negative points of view and oppositional attitudes (Eckert, 1989). Currently, this situation has become even more exacerbated as funding for education is cut and smaller schools are being closed down. The remaining schools are increasing in student population on a daily basis.

How are children viewed?

Not only do negative attitudes exist on the part of students towards the school system and its internal structures, but the reverse is also true. The question of how adults, teachers, parents, principals, and the society and culture as a whole view "kids" is also of concern. Lloyd deMause documents how the hatred of children was endemic in many early societies in which children were "killed, abandoned, battered, terrorized, sexually abused, and used for the emotional needs of adults" (p. 240). The child has been hated in a variety of ways. For example, the hatred of parents toward the individuating child when they become envious of the child flourishing while they feel unhappy, or when they view their children as burdens and impediments to freedom.

Even though current child-rearing practices reflect a vast improvement on those of previous centuries in nearly all cultures of the world, we still have a long way to go, as the hatred of children is still very evident in many of society's institutions as well as in our relationships with children. A reflection of this is found also on a global level. Children are often seen as burdensome nuisances, consciously malicious and difficult, or rebellious and destructive. The attitudes in schools reflect these beliefs too. Rules and regulations are structured to keep youth in check, reflecting the belief that if given more freedom their "evil" natures and inherent destructiveness would create havoc. In the drive to increasingly contain youth, the pressure upon them to be appropriate and conform also increases, contributing toward more aggressive behaviours in their reaction to adult's expectations. As deMause explains:

> "children throughout history have arguably been more vital, more gentle, more joyous, more curious, more courageous and more innovative than adults. Yet adults throughout history have routinely called children beasts, sinful, greedy, arrogant, lumps of flesh, vile, polluted, enemies, and fiends" (p. 242).

The vestiges of this kind of thinking are evident today in the mistrustful ways in which youth and their behaviours are often approached. It would seem that these kinds of attitudes permeate the world of children and adolescents, contributing to experiences of low self-esteem, depression, hatred, rebellion, retaliation, and violence.

The lack of interest in children in our society has led to their knowing that they are not honoured. As society continues to locate its disorders in the child, children begin to feel like rats in a maze. As they are taught coping behaviours or are medicated, they are forced to adjust to the madness of the maze, thus destroying the things that call to them and give them wings. Their fantasies become trapped in society's expectations of them and in society's emphasis on material possessions as they strive for achievement and perfection. As long as society continues to ignore the things that inspire children, the more it extinguishes their light. With the amount of violence in the world why then is it a surprise that schools reflect that violence, too? (James Hillman, personal communication, March 2005).

Attitudes and goals of education

In the modern school situation, the aim of education has become the development of rational mind, namely the acquisition of scientific knowledge and objective reasoning. Through education students are expected to gain a wide range of theoretical knowledge, highly developed powers of reasoning, and the qualities of objectivity and emotional distance (Martin 2005, p. 198). This split between reason and emotion epitomizes the separation of mind from body, head from hand, thought from action, and self from other that psychologist and educational reformer John Dewey (Dewey, 1916) spent many years trying to draw attention to in his attempt to unify education. Not only have these dichotomies emerged as the educational system has advanced, but, according to Michael Lerner (Lerner, 2000) contemporary schooling teaches students that their own success depends on their ability to do better than others, thus further eliminating a sense of connection to others and exacerbating the alienation already experienced in other ways. One of these other ways most decried by Lerner is the use of the Scholastic Aptitude Test (SAT), which negates the ability of the individual to be creative, caring, and connected to deep truths in literature, art, and philosophy. Instead the SAT measures the capacity to think in a mechanistic way under highly competitive circumstances, divorced from human understanding and meaningful thought. This serves as a blueprint for the strong emphasis on academic skills and achievements in education today. In the late 1990s, President Clinton endorsed public school choice and chartering as long as every school could be measured by one high standard, namely whether children learn what they need to know to compete and win in the global economy (Purpel 2000, p. 183).

As a connection continues to be made between academic achievement and economic success, school curricula increase in size and requirements for graduation rise, further alienating students from developing a true love of learning and inquiry. Instead, the joy in learning is substituted with pressure to reach higher and higher standards in order to be recognized. Schools are now generally judged on the basis of the students' academic achievement largely determined by standardized scores. Parent training and community support are virtually absent in schools, which are themselves struggling to cope with the pressures of the education and economic systems, and can barely educate their own teachers on what students need for support. This hardly provides an atmosphere conducive to the cultivation of community spirit or inclusiveness. In fact, students interviewed drew attention to how the ever-increasing emphasis on achievement and success in schools has resulted in less and less meaningful focus on community and respect for others (Shapiro 2005, p. 164). Rewarding experiences in school are often available only to students who perform well academically. Students who do not meet expectations in academic areas are denied access to rewards in other areas such as athletics, thus further alienating them (Gottfredson & Gottfredson, 1985). It is thus clear how students become alienated not only from an inherent curiosity and expansion of their own sense of self through a meaningful exploration of knowledge, but also from others in the quest for higher grades stemming from competition and achievement.

As the emphasis on test scores and standards has grown, the curriculum offered in most schools has become more standardized and conventional, offering a rather limited selection of what may be studied. This leaves students with little autonomy to make choices according to what inspires them or best fits their own temperaments. According to Amy Gutmann, "a just educational authority must not bias children's choices, but it must provide every child with an opportunity to choose freely and rationally" (Gutmann 1999, p. 34). She stresses the danger of the professional autonomy of teachers and school structures denying students any influence in shaping the form or content of their own education. In schools where teachers share authority with students over a wide range of decisions, students report a care about learning and a real sense of community. Such things as critical thinking, education for personal expression, education for social responsibility, interdisciplinary studies, environmental education, and so on, have been abolished from most curricula, further alienating students from their natural inclinations and interests (Purpel, 2000, p. 187). These dynamics detract from emphasis on traditions of teacher autonomy, community involvement, and student participation.

Counter-culture and students' rights

In the 1960s, along with the birth of the Cultural Revolution and counter-culture, demands for political and economic democracy extended to public schools. Demands for change in the school setting included an increase in emphasis on student creativity, imagination, and critical thinking, along with active participation in decision-making processes by students, parents, and the community as a whole. Due to the costs incurred by the Vietnam War and associated public issues at that time, funds were funnelled away from the public school system and the drive for more democratically structured schools lost its impetus.

Moving into the new millennium, as students' rights were increasingly overlooked, the division between assigned roles in the school system became more entrenched. The idea of belonging to a coherent community of interests, where decisions were made through democratic deliberation, was often abandoned altogether. Gradually local control of schools fell away and by 2003 virtually all school curriculum decisions could be overridden and/or imposed on by the dictates of the Bush administration. Teacher education programs as well as school structures and curricula were standardized and continue to be controlled by the federal government.

As incidences of school violence increased, more rules and restrictions were imposed on students, thus further reducing student rights and autonomy. It has been shown that curtailing students' freedom in an attempt to address violence within schools exacerbates the violence rather than reducing it (Pardeck, 2001). These days even young elementary students are suspended or expelled for bringing anything sharp such as a penknife to school, resulting in an intensification of feelings of rejection. The ABC News Channel's program on school violence (1999) suggests that the installation of metal detectors and such devices may incite students to commit more violence as an act of rebellion, particularly when inclusion, recognition, and acknowledgement is their need and hope. Schools have adopted a zero tolerance for any kind of potentially violent expression, which in turn has intensified the problem as these kinds of emotions become repressed, and increasingly have no milieu in which to be expressed. Findings indicate that disruption is greater in schools in which teachers express punitive views and actions as compared to those schools in which teachers express attitudes implying that students and parents should be included in how the school is run (Gottfredson & Gottfredson, 1985).

It becomes clear how policies such as these have eroded all levels of the school system, strongly influencing the existence of democratic choice on the part of all those involved. The organization of the school, the selection of administrative and educational content, as well as the teaching itself, illustrate how progress in democratically founded institutional structures has been short-circuited. The increasing use of police-like disciplinary tactics contributes to the climate of alienation in North America's schools, constellating violent tendencies. The climate of control found in most schools has a dramatic effect on students contributing to anxiety, depression, disempowerment, and rebellious or destructive behaviour.

Democracy in schools

Schools clearly lack a democracy that could permeate the whole institution. Deliberation and decision-making carried out in a democratic way would thrive on diversity, and would require discussion and dialogue in order to flourish. Adults would play a role in modelling and fostering a participatory style vital in sustaining democratic principles in educational settings. This in turn would be closely allied with individual development and a focus on catering to individual needs throughout systemic structures, policies, and philosophy. According to Gutmann (Gutmann, 1999), in the judgment of many critics of public schools in the United States, the record in teaching democratic virtue ranges from disappointing to disastrous. Critics have ample evidence to support their charges—public school systems in this country have engaged in educationally unnecessary tracking, they have presided over racial segregation in schools and classrooms, and they have instituted some of the most intellectually deadening methods of teaching that one might imagine (p. 65).

Students

Violence is a consequence of students being in an institutional context in which they have no choice and in which they are exposed to forces and directives over which they have no control (Fallis and Opotow, 2003). Encouraging students to air their feelings and describe their experiences, making sure they understand they have been heard, will not only help them to learn to express themselves effectively, but also support them in their relatedness to others within the school system in creative and constructive ways. Having more choice in how classes are structured and in the development of their own curricula will empower students. Receiving guidance and mentorship from teachers will encourage a sense of belonging.

Teachers

Teachers also feel alienated on a number of levels, namely within the system, among each other, and from the students. The professional responsibility of teachers is to uphold the principle of non-repression by cultivating within the students the capacity for democratic deliberation. This might call on teachers to resist the larger educational structures' dominant emphases such as SAT-oriented learning and, instead, instil an ability in their students to think critically and explore ideas intellectually in their own ways (Gutmann, 1999). As previously noted, due to increasing pressure for achievement in a particular way—namely, scores on structured tests such as the SAT and other tests imposed by the *No Child Left Behind Act* signed into law by President Bush in 2002—this opportunity mostly falls away for teachers who are obliged to school their students in expected ways. This alienates teachers from the inherent meaning and philosophy of teaching and what may have been initially their own ideals and hopes for education.

In order to support democratic deliberation among students, teachers should be sufficiently connected to their communities in order to understand the issues students bring with them to school. Unfortunately, this is largely not the case in present-day schools, where workload and resultant time constraints prohibit most teachers from knowing much about their students or their communities in a personal way. Most teachers who begin with a sense of intellectual mission lose it after several years of teaching, and either continue to teach in an uninspired, routine way or leave the profession to avoid intellectual stultification and emotional despair (p. 77). With the strong emphasis on discipline and avoidance of conflict, teachers are mainly seen as technicians enforcing the structures of the system. Teachers in turn have little control over the subject matter they present, and like students, little choice about what they offer in the classroom. They suffer low pay, low social status, and, in most public schools, difficulty in developing a positive sense of professionalism. Little attention is given to teachers' needs for support and acknowledgement, and like students, an appropriate context to air feelings, needs and ideas is mostly absent.

Students, teachers and violence

Teachers also experience a variety of indignities in schools ranging from rare but serious offences such as rape or assault, to more frequent, pervasive experiences of verbal abuse. Forty-eight percent of junior and senior high school teachers reported that students swore or made obscene gestures at them, 12% reported that they were threatened with physical injury, and another 12% that they were afraid to confront misbehaving students for fear of their own safety (Gottfredson & Gottfredson, 1985). Research results imply that school characteristics, including staffing, size, resources, plus educational and social climate, make a difference in the amount of teacher victimization in the school. The greater the teaching resources, the smaller the school, the less punitive teachers' attitudes, the more proficiency in teaching, and the more sensible the disciplinary measures, the less teacher victimization will be experienced. It seems that all of these qualities are rapidly deteriorating in the present-day public school system, resulting in a higher incidence of teacher victimization and alienation. The amount of students rotating through classes taught by different teachers also influences levels of teacher/student engagement. When teachers are involved in the education of large numbers of different students without sustained contact with them on a daily basis, the educational climate is impersonal and leads to disruption. This again highlights the importance of the personal bond between members of the system in creating meaningful relationships and a sense of inclusiveness and community.

In a study collecting over 1000 teachers' reports of aggressive incidents in the classroom or school setting, reports cover a range of behaviours such as rules violations, physical threats, fights, attacks on teachers, and group aggression (Goldstein, Palumbo, Striepling & Voutsinas, 1995). Results suggest a number of interventions, both verbal and physical, for teachers to use in these instances, whereby students' behaviour can be either curtailed or be physically restrained. In these authors' documentation of some of these incidents, it becomes clear that rather than addressing the underlying dynamics that initially cause the disruptive behaviour, thus preventing further occurrences, the focus in schools is placed on restricting students and their behaviour, and implementing harsher rules and limits for the future. Teachers are therefore trained to impose these measures in the classroom situation, rather than educated about how to establish rapport with students and provide an environment wherein problems can be discussed and shared. The teacher's obligation to be watchful about potentially aggressive behaviour and to maintain the readiness to intervene places a further strain on the teacher/student relationship, further inhibiting the freedom of expression of teachers. This is another aspect of the alienation that occurs for the teacher in the school situation that also has an impact on bonding with students as well as community building. This, of course, also increases the student's own experience of feeling alienated from teaching staff.

Teachers are also known to perpetrate violent acts such as some type of emotional attack on a student, a denigration of a student's work, a particularly harsh attitude, singling out of particular students for negative attention, or even, as has occurred in the past in various cultures, physical punishment ranging from a slap on the hand with a ruler to severe caning on the buttocks. The degree of violence in the media, domestic violence, torture in prisons, harsh treatment of enemies during war, and so on, all reflect the violence that occurs on all levels of society and culture. It could therefore be assumed that the experience of alienation and the possibility of violent expression arising from it are integral parts of human nature, and a distinct possibility in all sectors of society. This idea will be explored in more depth in following chapters.

Summary

The above review provides literary evidence of alienation and violence in schools, giving a statistical, historical, and socio-political overview of factors occurring on many levels within the school system. Social and cultural factors such as emphasis on perfectionism, freedom of choice, dislike of children, and teachers' difficulties, has opened the topic of alienation. This is explored in further depth in the next chapters. Concerning alienation, it has been shown that youth perpetrators of violence feel alienated from parents as well as other adults in their communities, and have difficulty expressing their experiences. The research also shows that ostracism breeds violence in return, particularly in the cases of school shootings. Many shooters had been either bullied or excluded from peer groups. Most youth lack trust in the ability of adults to do anything about bullying situations, and this perception leads to hopelessness, apathy, or revenge. The political movement of the school system away from individual attention to students toward a standardized method of educating and testing, has left an ever-widening gap in relationship interactions among students, teachers, and administrators, resulting in additional alienation and hostility.

In attempting to address bullying and school violence, emphasis is usually placed on the experience of the victims, whereas the perpetrators are summarily dismissed through punishment or imprisonment. Few attempts have been made to explore the psychology of the perpetrators themselves, and little is known about the internal dynamics they experience. A lack of awareness also exists concerning the perpetration of school violence as a reflection of repressed or denied violent tendencies existing as part of human nature.

CHAPTER TWO

Depth psychology and school violence

The material offered in this chapter will begin the journey into the underlying depths hidden beneath the overt behaviours described as school aggression and violence. In this section we will be looking at the connections between experiences of violence and expressions of psyche. Individual and cultural contexts will be explored. Although depth psychological concepts are introduced here, I want to reassure the reader that this book is not about depth psychology. It is about the underlying dynamics of school violence. I have found the best tools for exploring these dynamics in aspects offered by various depth psychological approaches. This chapter is an introduction to some of these methods, and in particular those that can assist us in delving more deeply into the more unknown aspects of school violence and related experiences. An understanding of the concepts and tools mentioned in this chapter will enable the reader to better follow the case studies and analysis that are presented later.

The origins of depth psychology

What is depth psychology? This term was first used a little over a century ago by Eugen Bleuler, Swiss psychiatrist and contemporary of Freud and Jung, to refer to the varied experiences found within the unconscious depths of individuals' psyches. Depth psychology is the study of that which is not accessible to direct observation. It moves from what is revealed to what is concealed. Throwing light upon unconscious material and bringing it to awareness makes conscious what was previously unknown. The process is one of diving into the unknown, into secrets, in order to reveal their existence and content. In order to get to the depths of the psyche, some dwelling with, and openness to phenomena that present themselves is required. In ancient religious disciplines, such as those found in the Orient and Greece, the existence of "depths" within the person was recognized as the basis of spiritual experience. This recognition led to a variety of spiritual practices and doctrines. In Europe and Western civilization however, the idea of the *unconscious depths* of the personality has mainly been used as a conceptual, intellectual tool for explaining the phenomena of the psyche.

Until Freud's time the notion of the unconscious was a general concept used to refer to deeper mechanisms underlying the conscious mind. Freud, however, through dream analysis and the use of interpretation crystallized this idea into a definite concept, useful in clarifying some of the confusion around human behaviour and personality. In finding a way to plumb the unconscious, Freud made the idea of depth psychology come alive in practice (Progoff, 1956). From the creative contributions of Freud, Jung and many other depth-oriented theorists, a psychological science of depth has emerged and continues to grow and develop.

Depth psychological concepts applicable to school violence

Telos

A particular meaning or purpose is perceived as occurring within symptomatic behaviour, expressions of the personality, or events. Each symptom or disturbance is believed to have some final purpose or meaning inherent in it, which is often beyond the perception of the observer. This is known as the teleological perspective or *telos*. In order to access this meaning, the disturbance needs to be explored and unravelled in order for it to give up its secrets. Secrets when explored often wake us up to the nature of parts of ourselves that are waiting to be recognized so that they can emerge and be integrated into the everyday life of the individual or society. When we react to cases of school violence on a superficial level, we want to abolish it, punish the perpetrators, and introduce structures that will prevent it from recurring. These measures do not appear to eradicate the problems. They are enforced in many schools and yet school violence still persists. However, if we can bring our attention to the tendency for violence, take time to access its deeper layers, we can find a wealth of meaning within it.

Freud

Freud, one of the fathers of depth psychology, believed that neurosis occurs when unacceptable material is repressed, becomes unconscious, and can no longer be contained in this state (Wyss, 1973). Repressed material, often instinctive, is held in the unconscious due to its rather distinctive nature potentially posing a threat to the identified ego (Gay, 1989). A censorship process maintains the repression and keeps this material in the unconscious. However, this repressed material is not completely cut off but does express itself through instinctual behaviour. Due to repression, perceptions cannot be experienced as sensations directly, but can emerge as physical pain or other neurotic symptoms.

The ego, representing reason and common sense, seeks to bring the influence of the external world to bear upon the instinctive passions of the individual. This reasonable part of the ego, known as the superego, exerts pressure on the individual to act in accord with family and cultural norms or expectations. Those impulses that fall outside of what is considered acceptable to the superego, become repressed. It is when the repression becomes so intolerable due to its extreme content or magnitude that the content bursts the barriers of the superego to emerge in extreme behaviour or neurotic symptoms. To some degree, therefore, the ego becomes powerless in the face of the more unknown and uncontrollable forces that are part of the instinctual forces, including the material repressed by the superego (Gay, 1989). The repressed material, however, can be addressed and brought to consciousness in order to restore psychic balance. In exploring the contents of the unconscious through dreams and associations, meaning is found within presenting symptoms. The teleological perspective here concerns the liberation of repressed material, making it accessible to the conscious mind. When liberation does not occur, unconscious forces may exert strong influences upon the ego causing disruptive, disturbing, and possibly destructive behaviour. When liberation does occur there is more ability to make the repressed material useful as one feels more in charge of it, rather than it's possession.

Jung

Jung also placed emphasis on the teleological perspective stating that the psychic process, like any other life process, is not just a causal sequence, but also a process with a teleological orientation

> "Life is teleology *par excellence*; it is the intrinsic striving towards a goal, and the living organism is a system of directed aims which seek to fulfil themselves. The end of every process is its goal. Youthful longing for the world and for life, for the attainment of high hopes and distant goals, is life's obvious teleological urge which at once changes into fear of life, neurotic resistances, depressions and phobias if at some point it remains caught in the past, or shrinks from risks without which the unseen goal cannot be attained" (Jung, 1927, p. 405).

Closely connected to the above ideas is Jung's exploration of the individuation process, a teleological perspective of the psyche's unfolding of greater awareness of the deeper layers of the self, so that a "knowing" of levels of unconscious material can occur for the individual on his life path. Jung describes individuation as a regulating principle acting as an integrative, unifying power, drawing attention to its presence through dream images and symbols.

> "When universal laws of human fate break in upon the purposes, expectations and opinions of the personal consciousness,

these are stations along the road of the individuation process. This process is, in effect, the spontaneous realization of the whole man. The inevitable one-sidedness of our conscious life is continually being corrected and compensated by the universal human being in us, whose goal is the ultimate integration of conscious and unconscious, or better, the assimilation of the ego to a wider personality" (p. 292).

Consciousness is influenced by the unconscious, and as one becomes more aware of the unconscious, one becomes more conscious of who one truly is. This process increases the choices one makes about being in this world; however, if the unconscious is unattended to, it will unconsciously live out one's life for one. Disturbance will happen to us in order to cultivate awareness of facets of psyche trying to become integrated into the conscious mind. As aspects of the unconscious arise to consciousness, they become differentiated into polarities, entrenching themselves in the ego. The teleological aspect of this process is found in the birthing of awareness of previously unknown aspects of the unconscious. When one is unable to volitionally pick up aspects of the unconscious that are calling to one through dream symbols, physical and psychological symptoms, synchronicities, and collective phenomena, these will manifest of their own accord, seeking finality in the fulfilment of their lived nature.

Essentially, Jung's ideas here are similar to those of Freud's, in that unconscious material is brought to the conscious mind in order to relieve symptoms. Freud's approach rests very much upon the freeing of repressed material, whereas Jung places more emphasis on the restoration of the nature or essence of life as an impulse of the deepest layers of psyche. The process whereby this occurs involves an exploration of individual psyche, although Jung incorporated the idea of the collective unconscious and its array of archetypes as also exerting a teleological influence.

Both Freud and Jung's ideas can be used to access more meaning in experiences from which we usually shy away, or which horrify us. We may well ask, "what is being repressed that finds expression through primitive instinctual disruptions; what is trying to come to consciousness through this symptomatic behaviour"? Some answers to these questions lie in the chapters ahead as we continue to explore the psychology of the school disturber and the social context in which she exists.

Hillman

Hillman attempts to reconnect depth psychology to the mythical perspective held within the images of soul, which perspective he claims lies at the base of any psychology. Rather than view only the personal experiences of the individual, he also makes reference to cultural phenomena, and finds it important to open to the richness of the pantheon of Gods or archetypes they include. He asserts this as a kind of "religious passion in a culture where personalism confines passion to 'my' emotions, inside my private developmental history and my own body" (Hillman1975, p. xi). He stresses that the study of psyche must not only rest on the personal, but must embody the perspectives of the images that are closely connected to soul.

For Hillman, meaning emerges through this connection when the *imaginal* represents itself through one's experience of it. He identifies *daimons*, powers, and personified principles that make up the mythical patterns of the unconscious, as the very patterns that rule humans, even though humans may be unconscious of them. These archetypes form the structures of one's consciousness as if they were Gods creating of themselves:

> "The soul is less an object of knowledge than it is a way of knowing the object, a way of knowing knowledge itself. Prior to any knowledge are the psychic premises that make knowledge possible at all, and all knowing may be examined in terms of these psychic premises" (*ibid* p. 131).

Hillman suggests here an archetypal theory of knowing in which a style of thought expresses an archetypal mode of consciousness, including its style of behaviour. The teleological aspect of his approach embodies coming to know the archetypes while consciously perceiving through their eyes, sensing through their bodies as if they exist through us and we exist through them. An understanding of how to do this allows psyche to manifest through one's awareness of it. This theory invites us to explore behaviour as instinctual expressions of archetypal forces. It offers ways in which to embody the energy of the archetypes in order to consciously give them expression and gain knowledge from them.

Depth psychology asserts that what is not admitted into awareness erupts in disturbing ways, reflecting the precise qualities that consciousness is trying to avoid due to their negative associations. These eruptions may occur through dream images, fantasies, and symptoms. Freud declared that the unconscious is revealed only in pathological material. Hillman echoes this when he states that psyche is found in the disturbance, the difference, the craziness and deviance, held internally in one's relationship with oneself and expressed in daily life and moments of crisis. In embracing these as gateways into soul, one is fulfilling the purpose the gods intended for one. In being able to embrace these mysteries as teachers—as guides along the path of consciousness—one embarks on a journey leading one into greater knowledge and awareness (*ibid* p. 70). For example, exploring the behavioural expressions of perpetrators of violence within the school system cultivates insight into the disturbance. Through unfolding the symptomatic behaviour, the meaning or instinctual tendency that lies within this disturbing behaviour will emerge allowing the individual and the collective to transform and integrate its deeper meaning. This expands the available repertoire of awareness and behaviour.

Weinstein and platt

Weinstein and Platt endeavour to illustrate the usefulness of various aspects of psychoanalytic theory in the development of sociological theory. They stress the interaction between individuals and groups as vital for an understanding of the flexibility of individual personality, as well as the ability to analyze it. They point out the degree to which psychoanalytic thinking lacks this focus, devaluing external influences in the world (Weinstein & Platt, 1973). In their writings they attempt to show that any network of relationships constitutes a context of psychic support giving meaning to situations, and that identity is comprised of such relationships (p. 16). Personal psychic processes interact with one another but are also in direct exchange with culture and society. Social stability or change therefore impacts individual psychic processes. Personal stability thus depends to the greatest degree upon the continued integrity of the social order. Revolutionary acts decry the brutality, senselessness, exploitation, and oppression of a system or society. The revolutionary is not deterred by threats of punishment but is compelled to make a statement against present structure, pushing for change in the social fabric. Future developments in the psychoanalytic field, according to these authors, must be in the direction of greater recognition and understanding of social and cultural influences on individual psychology, recasting psychoanalytic propositions in psychosocial terms. How relevant their view is to the field of school violence! We have already seen in chapter one how social and cultural influences interweave in the co-creation of individual behaviours within the functioning of the school system.

Mindell

Mindell developed the concept of the *city shadow* as holding the repressed and unrealized aspects of all people (Mindell, 1988). He suggests that we are just learning about the forces and effects which move people, and that those who manifest unusual behaviours which disturb us can show us the way to more understanding of the human process. The disturbance becomes an awakener for the individual and the culture in which he or she lives. Information can be found within it that addresses cultural and global symptoms, ushering in greater awareness of the growth and integration that may occur if the path of nature were to be followed with more attention. Following nature implies a process-oriented view of experience as a flow of energy, equivalent to "the way" of Taoism or the path along which all things move (Mindell, 1985). Nature manifests itself through psychic phenomena such as dream figures, mythical events, symptoms, relationship, and world events, all of which hold information that can be brought to awareness for the growth of consciousness on individual and global levels.

Disturbers of a collective identity might be meaningful for the society and city in which they live, but as with any *identified patient*, there is a great resistance to acknowledging this because it might call for change on a collective level, rather than placing the responsibility on a small sector of the population. In broadening the societal attitude to those presenting cultural symptomatology, and exploring systemic and cultural factors attributing to the disturbance, the *identified patient* is freed of his burden, which is then held and processed by the communal family (Mindell, 2000).

Summary

The above section briefly touches on some of the teleological aspects of the work of depth psychologists. This is a rather reduced glimpse into the philosophical, sociological and psychological premises that touch on the topic of disturbance. The idea of *telos* as an aspect of depth psychology is emphasized because this aspect has been entirely disregarded in the search for solutions to the problem of school violence. Moreover, the perpetration of school violence generally is not viewed as representing something meaningful trying to emerge from a deeper level of awareness. In addressing these problems from a depth orientation, a different lens through which to view school problems is offered. This allows for the possibility of new inspiration, fostering increased understanding among individuals, communities, and societies with regard to the problems of alienation and violence within the school system.

CHAPTER THREE

New ideas on school alienation and violence

In this chapter I will be using composite case material taken from personal interactions with adolescent groups and individual clients to illustrate psychological factors existing on individual and collective levels. Theoretical views will be introduced from a Jungian perspective and linked to behavioural dynamics and interventions made. Concepts and experiential factors explored here bring increased understanding of the role of the school avenger, and what transpires to constellate that role in the school field. Material that is usually held secret is revealed from the perspective of the adolescent, and interventions mentioned are those that help to contain the disavowed experiences, creating a place where they can be shared and processed.

Jungian perspectives and interventions

The shadow

I have been working with groups of adolescents at a local high school facilitating dialogue, processing dreams, and using exercises to support the growth of self-awareness and individuation. Whereas very reticent at first, group members have begun to speak a little more openly about their home lives, their relationships with their parents, siblings, and each other, their school situation, their views on life, and very hesitantly about their inner experiences. The group is slowly becoming a *temenos*; a "sacred precinct"; a sacrosanct place impenetrable to threat to those within its boundaries (Jung, 1911). As group members begin to feel safer and more contained, they are less reluctant to share their thoughts and feelings. Here is a description of one of our meetings.

> *I am facilitating a group of 8 adolescent males and females all over the age of 15. We have been working together once a week for the past three months. The group discussion today turns to parties. Hilarity breaks out as people share outrageous stories of their own or others' deeds while "high" either on drugs, alcohol, or on party atmosphere. As the discussion progresses, some members describe fights breaking out in the midst of partying. The group becomes more solemn. There are pauses, moments of silence. In one such hush, Gwen begins to speak. She tells of how she used to physically fight other girls and wanted to kill them. She still hates people and often feels murderous. She is trying to curb her anger and hatred, and has succeeded in stuffing it deep down, she says. Sometimes it explodes and she finds herself physically attacking somebody she dislikes. This gets her into trouble with authority. She prefers to keep her feelings bottled up and doesn't want others to know what she is really thinking and feeling. She doesn't want to get into trouble any more. She has been given a number of warnings for violent behaviour and feels threatened to be on her best behaviour. Then in almost an aside she confides that she is on medication for depression.*
>
> *Gwen's sharing in the group makes a space for others to divulge their inner secrets. One girl who is slovenly and overweight begins to talk about how much she hates people. "In fact", she says, "I would like to kill nearly everyone I know. I hate people!" she says with great passion. This is a young woman who sat beyond the edges of the group for many weeks, usually in a corner. Previously made fun of by her peers in the larger school context, she has now gained the respect of other group members for her rather extreme views.*
>
> *After these two statements, there is a hush in the group. Some participants are looking down as though in deep feeling. We had not*

previously spoken of the desire to kill. This is a new topic for the group.
A young man turns to me. "This will stay just among us?" he asks,
making sure that our confidentiality policy is still in place. Violence is
taboo in the school.

Aggressive and violent feelings are forced to go underground in
a culture that both represses and punishes their expression. Not
only are they disallowed in terms of outer expression, but within
the internal worlds of these kids they are kept under lock and key.
Being able to talk about thoughts and feelings of this kind is hugely
relieving to the individual and the whole field, especially when
there is a dark cloud of secrecy and repression hanging over the
topic. Usually there is a great deal of shame and guilt that accom-
panies these kinds of feelings and impulses, further prohibiting
expression of this kind. Shame can be alleviated when finding
out that others also share these experiences and that one is not a
pariah because there may be murderous thoughts in one's fantasy
life. Shame and guilt lead to repression of expression on both personal and cultural levels, developing further what is known as the
shadow.

The shadow is defined as those elements, feelings, emotions, ideas,
and beliefs with which we do not identify and which are repressed
due to education, culture, or value system (Guggenbuhl-Craig,
1990). It is everything that has been rejected during the development of the personality because it did not fit into the ego ideal.
The shadow is co-created by a number of different forces including personal experiences, traumatic incidents, parental upbring-
ing, school education, enculturation, and moral/religious precepts
found within cultures. When the individual personally represses
particular psychic contents, the shadow is primarily personal; when
a sub-culture or culture is responsible for the repression it is primarily collective. Collectively, the shadow can be seen as an archetype, having a potential for behaviour present from the beginning
and closely related to the instincts. Shadow material is something
we react to in others but often cannot recognize in ourselves. To
become conscious of it involves recognizing the dark aspects of
the personality as present and real (Jung, 1951). Even when shown
these parts by others, it can be very difficult to acknowledge them
and even more challenging to integrate them back into the whole

personality. The material constituting the shadow has an emotional nature, almost an autonomy, which results in affect happening to the individual, rather than the individual initiating that emotion herself. These emotions are mostly unrecognized and usually uncontrolled, stemming from the unconscious, and when they burst out one is "not only the passive victim of affects, but also singularly incapable of moral judgment" (*ibid* p. 9). Gwen's description of how her anger sometimes takes over with the result that she finds herself in a fight, while trying her best to keep her anger bottled up, alludes to the shadow of aggression. This is both a personal phenomenon for her, but is also reflected in her culture, where children from a young age are taught that aggression is not "good" and should therefore not be experienced or expressed (Guggenbuhl, 1997).

There is usually resistance to becoming conscious of shadow material and attempts to integrate it into the ego identity are not always successful. When faced with previously unconscious parts of the self, one tends to experience discomfort, shame, guilt, and defensiveness. These resistances usually go along with projections in which the disavowed aspects, both personal and archetypal, are projected onto others, often resulting in criticism of the other, stereotyping, discrimination, racial hatred, and war.

> "The effect of projection is to isolate the individual from his environment due to the illusory nature of the relationship that forms. Projections change the world into the replica of one's own unknown face. In the last analysis, therefore, they lead to an autoerotic or autistic condition in which one dreams a world whose reality remains forever unattainable. The resultant *sentiment d'incompletude* and the still worse feeling of sterility are in their turn explained by projection as the malevolence of the environment, and by means of this vicious circle the isolation is intensified" (Jung, 1959, p. 9).

Adolescents suffering difficulties in relationship become more and more alienated by the projections heaped upon others until at last the resultant hatred of their projections on a collective level cannot be held in any longer and expresses in an act of destruction. Projections can be either individual as in the ascribing of evil to particular other people, or collective, personifying evil as a collective entity, when *life* or the *world* become the Enemy. This is exemplified in the following example.

> *On another occasion in the group, Derek arrives for the group meeting in a foul mood. Derek is usually a loner, and suffers from a sense of inadequacy, usually overlaid by bravado about his abilities. Today he is very threatening to other group members, derisive and snarling, and at one point gets right in my face talking over me. He is muttering about his parents, his teachers, and some of his peers. According to him they are vindictive and hateful, never appreciating or acknowledging him, often putting him down in a mean way.*
>
> *Trying to support him by acknowledging his point of view and taking his side goes nowhere and his behaviour continues to cycle. Attempting to represent the "hateful" role in the group also gets no response from him. As he gets louder and more threatening, one of the girls shares that she knew Derek had used meth earlier that morning. Derek has a history of drug abuse. It is a rule in the group that no member can participate if they are "high" on something and Derek, who grudgingly attends group sessions, has managed so far to avoid indulging. However, today he has succumbed to his addictive pattern, and as a result, is aggressive and threatening to others in the group. In worrying that he will become physically violent, I ask him to leave the group. Derek leaves the room muttering to himself about how unfair this is as he has not done anything, and that it is all the fault of those f—ers out there.*

When the self is alienated, many of its aspects such as the shadow, retire into the background and remain beyond the realm of the conscious mind. Alienations of the self, in which the self is divested of its reality in favour of imposed external roles or fantasies, can lead to the collective taking precedence. This may correspond to a social ideal, duty and virtue, or on the other hand, the living out of primordial imagery usually not condoned by the social system. One can see how the qualities of the individual school avenger, acting from a position where shadow material lies beyond consciousness, are projected onto others in the environment. This dynamic is clearly noticed in Derek's attitude, where he finds others hateful while being hateful himself. In turn, the school and social systems mirror this dynamic of projection where shadow is projected onto individual school children who do not measure up to the standardized image of what a student should be like. These children often hold the projections of the system in which they live and as such may easily be stereotyped and scapegoated. However, the shadow is not intrinsically evil. Whatever is repressed and held in the shadow has a huge amount of energy, and if tapped can release a great deal of positive potential. It can support the unfolding of creative and life-supporting energy when it is revealed (Jung, 1951). The contents of shadow, when encouraged and supported, may be used for growth and evolution. It is when there is a refusal on the part of the ego, or the culture, to accept shadow contents that disturbance and upheaval may occur.

> *This week the kids have been invited to bring along musical instruments to group. We know that Derek is a guitarist as he has told us many times how good he is at guitar. We invite him to play for us. He introduces a song that he has written himself and launches into a heavy metal piece. The lyrics he has written embody the aggression the group experienced from him as described previously. However, in his music and words, behind the expressed aggression, lies a powerful statement of his views concerning power relationships. The violent tendencies he is usually prevented from showing seem to emerge in this case as a strong message against the abuse of power. His creative process has developed an outlet for repressed anger and has allowed its expression in a meaningful way.*
>
> *Derek receives positive feedback from others in the group about his music and song. In group discussion the strength of his lyrics and style of presentation are loudly acclaimed. During the ensuing weeks, I notice a change in the way Derek engages with others. He no longer appears tense and angry much of the time, becoming more congruent in his communications, abler to express his feelings more directly. He had taken a positive step along his path of individuation.*

The individuation process

The individuation process calls upon us to recognize unconscious material that emerges through instinctive expression, impulses, projections, dreams, symptoms, and synchronicities. The aim of individuation is to divest the self of the false wrappings of the persona on the one hand, and of the suggestive power of primordial images on the other (Jung, 1928). Individuation fulfils the peculiarity of one's own nature by supporting the definite, unique being one is.

> Individuation means becoming an "in-dividual," and, in so far as "individuality" embraces our innermost, last and incomparable uniqueness, it also implies becoming one's own self. We could therefore translate individuation as "coming to selfhood" or "self-realization" (p. 173).
>
> Not only is individuation a process of differentiation, having for its goal the development of the individual personality. Since the individual is not only a single entity, but also, by his very existence, presupposes a collective relationship, the process of individuation does not lead to isolation, but to an intenser and more universal collective solidarity (p. 155).

In divesting the self of its reality in favour of an external role, or an imagined or expectant fantasy, the self retires into the background and is taken over by either the imperative of social recognition, or a primordial image. In these cases collective considerations and obligations take over, often corresponding to a social ideal or an impulse from the collective unconscious. This results in self-alienation. In following a propensity for imitation ensuring social order and an acceptable persona, the uniformity of individuals' minds becomes intensified into an unconscious bondage to the environment. It therefore becomes difficult to find the truly individual in oneself, the authentic individual lying beneath the collective order.

Archaic symbolism such as that found in art, dreams, and fantasies, are collective factors, as are basic instincts and basic forms of thinking and feeling. A large amount of individual psychology is really collective, found in all universally agreed on, understood, and expressed phenomena. Through his contamination with others and the loss of a sense of self, the individual falls into situations, and commits actions that bring him into disharmony with himself (*ibid* p. 155). Individual traits, according to Jung, are almost completely overshadowed by the collective, and therefore it becomes extremely important to pay special attention to the delicacy of individuality if it is not to be smothered. This is just the dynamic that appears when the individual school child carries the burden of collective alienation and violence, resulting in a breakdown of the individual's ability to contain all that this implies. A good example of this is found in Gwen's description of herself as being murderous, but bottling up her feelings so as not to get into trouble. Her rage does burst out at times when she physically attacks others. At the same time, she is depressed and using medication to help her to feel "okay". To Jung it is imperative that we become conscious of ourselves through self-knowledge, widening our personal consciousness and bringing the individual into communion with the world at large (p. 178). In this way, we can also contribute to the growth of collective awareness through the individuation process, as deeper understanding of the individual process enables more awareness also for the collective. With more insight into the individual experience of the school offender we can also learn about where the system needs improvement.

Alienation and the longing for nurturing

While the archetypal mother figure offers containment and nourishment, the actual parenting situation rarely actualizes these to the degree that provides fulfilment for the longing for complete nurturing. There therefore exists an idealized parental image in realization of the hope for complete nurturing and acceptance. Due to the disappointment and insecurity suffered at the failure of the real mother or father to meet these expectations, the idealized imago replaces the image of the failed parent, holding within it all the qualities longed for by the child. The archetypal mother, together with the real parent in the form of the parent imago, symbolizes everything that functions as "mother" for the individual. In associating happiness and fulfilled longing for life with the mother imago, the individual is unable to support his own initiative, as well as his own abilities, to break through the challenges of the world. Instead, "he is crippled by the memory that the world and happiness may be had as a gift from the mother. The fragment of world which he must encounter again and again is never quite the right one, since it does not fall into his lap, does not meet him half way, but remains resistant, has to be conquered, and submits only to force" (Jung, 1951, p. 11). His initiative and staying power become immobilized through his belief that everything is attainable through the mother. In wanting to be enveloped and held by the mother, in staying loyal to her, he seeks the protection and nourishment that is unattainable in the world. This remains an illusion that he is forever seeking as he lives regressively from a psychological viewpoint, despite his desire to organize his world and live within it in a satisfying way. The imperfections of real life cannot compete with the state of inviolable fulfilment offered by the lure of the mother imago, taken to be the real mother. He becomes more removed from the real world while at the same time longing for engagement with it. The school child who encounters challenges within the school environment that she feels unable to meet, seeks protection from the real mother or parental figure, who on failing to provide the succour that is sought for by the child, exacerbates the child's attempt to hide within the folds of the mother imago's skirts. This further alienates the child from the reality of the world she is facing at school, as well as from her own capacity to overcome the obstacles presented, resulting in loss, disappointment, self-hatred, anger, and revenge.

This dynamic has been clearly illustrated in many cases where school shooters show increased social withdrawal with fearful, angry, or depressed mood becoming more evident (Moore et al. 2003). School shooters are generally viewed as being on the margins of social groups and see themselves as being either "loners" or not quite belonging or fitting in anywhere within the social fabric, despite their intense concern about their social standing in their school and among their peers. Shooters easily give up trying to affiliate with social groups when not included. A common factor is found among the shooters indicating falling school grades in months prior to the attack and a resultant change in school status.

> Gary had flunked all his classes in the prior school year and had been referred to a special program at his high school. He had also been reported to the school principal on a number of occasions for fighting with other boys during recess, and had been caught stealing a couple of times. He had been offered the opportunity to become part of a sports team when noticed for his natural ability and talent at this sport, but had dropped out of that about a year prior to joining our group. In group he is generally apart from most of the other children, in a depressed mood, and often complaining about the work load and the quality of teaching. He is also down on himself for not being smart

enough to get through school. In our group meetings he will often lie on the couch nestling his head into the lap of one of the girl participants who is his one close friend. He tends to gravitate toward her each week in the group and will often find a spot close to her, either on the couch or sitting side-by-side with her in chairs. He always makes physical contact of some kind with her, usually in a posture that allows him to receive some kind of nurturing contact. Gary idealizes his mother who is rather enmeshed with him, identities as his buddy, and idolizes him, at the same time trying to "fix" his life, but with problems of her own.

In referring to children and adolescents who engage in the activity of stealing, Donald Winnicott maintains that the child is looking for the sweetness that can be provided by the good mother. Without this loving sweetness, he becomes "more and more inhibited in love, and consequently more and more depressed and depersonalized, eventually being unable to feel the reality of things at all, except the reality of violence" (Winnicott, 1984, p.116). Winnicott differentiates love from sentimentality, which he refers to as the tendency to sacrifice everything for the "happiness" of the child, or the condition of indulgence. An unsentimental attitude however, reflects the appreciation "not so much of talent, as of the struggle behind all achievement, however small" (p. 91). In not receiving the "happiness" that comes with the appreciation for the authentic self, when searching for it in the world and not finding it, the child falls into a regressive state unable to construct an alternative way of encountering life. Destructiveness on inner or outer levels then occurs.

It is apparent that when the real parents fall short, children who attempt to cling to the idealized parent image in the hope of being able to deal with the world, may become disillusioned and angry. Their inability to "make it through" in ways expected of them, leads to tendencies to hold on even more tightly to the longing to be held by the mother imago. A repetitive cycle of recrimination, bitterness, and disappointment lead to a diminishment of the individual's ability to function. This in turn results in increased hostility toward the environment and all within it who are unable to provide the support, nourishment, and recognition desired. Acts such as stealing, fighting, as well as aggression towards teachers and other students may become common, causing concern to others within the school system.

Aggression

If we can begin with an assumption that aggression is a part of human nature and that pleasure in destruction and violence is an ancient, human quality, we can begin to make space for the shadow. Children can be helped to draw a distinction between natural aggression and violent fantasies, and other acts which would be considered unacceptable as outright harmful violent expression (Guggenbhul, 1997, p. 42). When children's natural tendencies to fantasize and express aggression through play are refused, disallowed, and reacted to with strong disapproval, the result may be an inner obligation to live these out in some way, to bring the repressed material out into the world in a somewhat amplified or distorted form. The more the disavowal and repression, the greater will be the symptomatic behaviour that results in the expression of violence as a shadow quality (Stein, 1995). The more we disavow or split off certain characteristics, the more they will become "loss of soul" (Storr, 1983, p. 217) and give rise to expressions that may be considered destructive or evil. Regulated aggression is essential for development and personal survival. One's capacity for self-defense ensures survival and needs to be supported in a life supporting way in the young child (Akhtar, Kramer & Parens 1995).

Those studying aggression and conflict in zoology and sociology, suppose that aggression and conflict are linked with survival in species, and so specifically rewarded in humans, that conflict will appear whenever the social system provides opportunities and approval for it (Hamburg, 1963). Humans are observed to learn and practice aggression more easily than most other species and to use aggressive routes to solve both interpersonal and international problems. Even though most of humankind does not readily identify with its tendency toward aggression, destructive behaviours abound in the world, and it is evident that a large part of humanity over a long period of time has enjoyed such things as torture, war and devastation of other people/s (Bell-Fialkoff, 1999). Aggression is favoured as a natural way of dealing with conflict, either internal or external, offered by natural laws of evolution, while at the same time it is demonized and disavowed on the social level. Alan Guggenbuhl suggests that we can be masters over our aggression by learning to use it skilfully rather than destructively. Jung might add that making aggressive tendencies conscious would support its teleological purpose and enable it to integrate into useful expression, thus linking it to the individuation process. As with any kind of shadow material, natural aggressive tendencies, when thwarted, manifest in a distorted form on the collective level.

Disturbers of a collective identity are generally shunned by that society. Acknowledging that their behaviour may be an important wake-up call on a more global level, is mostly resisted. School shooters, bullies, and others showing aggressive tendencies do disturb the status quo of the system. Those reacting to school violence attempt to eradicate the disturber, usually through expulsion, rather than explore where the disturber may be bringing something meaningful to the system itself. As already discussed, aggression and violence occur on many levels of the school system. In looking at violence more globally, aggression and violence can be noticed in all sectors of societies and cultures, although mostly denied, rationalized, or hidden. Individuals and groups often feel victimized by aggressive tendencies, viewing them as happening to them from a source outside themselves and beyond their control. There are many instances when aggression and/or violence erupt, such as in gang assaults, political advertising, warlord rivalries, and so on. Little provision is made for exploring intrapersonal or interpersonal aggression, which is generally frowned upon and made taboo.

Scapegoating

Humans generally see themselves as harmless, and while not denying that terrible things happen, individuals usually see the "other" as being responsible for the harm done.

> "Even if, juristically speaking, we were not accessories to the crime, we are always, thanks to our human nature, potential criminals. None of us stands outside humanity's black collective shadow. Whether the crime occurred many generations back or happens today, it remains the symptom of a disposition that is always and everywhere present—and one would therefore do

well to possess some "imagination for evil" for only the fool can permanently disregard the conditions of his own nature. In fact, this negligence is the best means of making him an instrument of evil, leading to the projection of the unrecognized evil into "the other". This strengthens the opponent's position in the most effective way, because the projection carries the *fear*, which we involuntarily and secretly feel for our own evil, over to the other side and considerably increases the formidableness of his threat. What is even worse, our lack of insight deprives us of the *capacity to deal with evil*. We should, so we are told, eschew evil and, if possible, neither touch nor mention it. For evil is also the thing of ill omen, that which is tabooed and feared. This apotropaic attitude towards evil, and the apparent circumventing of it, flatter the primitive tendency in us to shut our eyes to evil and drive it over some frontier or other, like the Old Testament scapegoat, which was supposed to carry the evil into the wilderness. It would be an insufferable thought that we had to take personal responsibility for so much guiltiness. We therefore prefer to localize the evil in individual "criminals" or "groups of criminals", while washing our hands in innocence and ignoring the general proclivity to evil" (Jung, 1946, p. 296).

In the above extract, Jung refers to the projection of evil on to others due to discomfort with one's own nature. In looking at the dynamic of scapegoating, it can be acknowledged that it is not only evil that is projected on others, but also a variety of qualities that are made taboo and thus disavowed as inherent tendencies in human nature. Aggression and violence are among these. This is best illustrated by a case example.

> Stella has been seeing me for therapy for a couple of weeks. She has been anxious and depressed, not wanting to go to school. She has said that the other kids are mean to her, constantly teasing her, and rejecting her from their social groups. Today her father comes into therapy with her to report that Stella has been expelled from school. She had taken a pocketknife with her to school and when surrounded and taunted by a group of kids, had pulled out the knife and threatened them with it. Stella is distraught. Through her sobs she tries to justify her actions. When she finally quietens down, I notice a change in her

posture and tone. Her eyes become steely, her jaw set, and in a strong
voice she says, "I'm glad that I did that—they deserved it. I'm glad
that I'll never see them again!"

In expelling Stella from school, she had been identified as the problem. The behaviour of the other children, their relentless persecution of Stella, and her apparent helplessness at their cruel treatment had not been addressed within the school system. She was seen to be the problem-maker, the disturber who had engaged in unacceptable behaviour delegated taboo at school. Stella became the scapegoat. Imbued with the violent tendencies and aggression denied by others, suffering from alienation after rejection by her peers, she was cast out of the school society in which she was hoping to find a place for herself. Does this leave the system free of aggression? By no means, and yet the belief is that in getting rid of the identified perpetrator, the system can then resume its apparently harmonious functioning. The suppurating unrest remains behind, while being overlooked or denied.

Sylvia Brinton Perera draws attention to the rituals surrounding the separation of the collective from evil through confession and sacrifice (Perera, 1986). The scapegoat rite purified and renewed the community through ritual slaughter or sacrifice. The evil recognized as lying within the members of the society was symbolically placed into the sacrificial offering and was then released for the collective through the sacrificial rite. In some cases the offering itself was honoured and revered by the tribe or community, and was chosen for certain qualities that inspired this honour. In other cases however, those chosen for sacrifice were seen to be alien, such as the physically deformed or retarded, members of minority groups, or those fallen out of favour. In this way the unacceptable or evil aspects of humanity were vanquished and expelled from daily life. Through ritual, man and woman were once again re-united with God and a higher existence in which a life of purity and integrity could be established. Perera's description of this rite aptly describes the process that occurred in Stella's school situation and explains the need to extradite the bearer of the perceived impurity from the community.

Stella's eventual delight and sense of regained power when she felt some satisfaction at taking out her knife and asserting herself, is also well described by Perera (1986) as follows. Scapegoated individuals have difficulty in distinguishing between power as an ego necessity and vengeful destructiveness. They therefore fear to wield any power at all, and it finally takes the form of aggressive and impulsive outbursts. Expressing power may provide moments of relief from the loneliness of feeling outcast, one's own sense of guilt and self-hatred, and suffering incurred by rejection. In these brief moments, the scapegoated individual may obtain a glimpse into what it is like to feel powerful. This was clearly the case with Stella, and her regained sense of power continued as she made choices around the next school she would attend.

Evil

A view that takes Guggenbuhl's acceptance of aggressive fantasies and impulses even further, embraces violence as an endemic part of humanity reflecting the qualities of God (Edinger, 1984; Jung 1934; Stein, 1995). Here violence is supported as a force of nature, the expression of a god or archetypal figure. Jung views both good and evil as principles. The word principle comes from "prius" meaning "that which is first," or "in the beginning". This leads to an understanding that good and evil as principles exist long before and far beyond that which can be comprehended. Jung mentions that the ultimate principle is God and therefore principles are simply aspects of God.

> "The spirit that penetrates all things, or shapes all things, is the World Soul. The soul of the world therefore is a certain only thing, filling all things, bestowing all things, binding and knitting together all things that it might make one frame of the world" (Jung,1934, p. 494).

Evil as an aspect of the devil is also identified with the figure of Lucifer, both the devil and Lucifer being viewed as aspects of God. Lucifer is a light bearer, bringing light into the darkness of the unconscious. Lucifer, meaning light bearer, is the bearer of consciousness, but is also synonymous with the devil. The devil therefore is viewed as an aspect of God bringing light into the darkness.

Imagine coming into the school situation with a view that is able to embrace expressions of the individual as principles, either "good" or "bad", as well as pathways to God. This belief would support the unravelling of acts of aggression and violence as an illuminating path of action, bringing us closer to the meaning of the self and its process toward individuation (God). With this view, a place can be made in which disturbing tendencies can be explored in order to find where they may indeed be bringing a light-bearing message.

Evil is the result of conscious material being relegated to the unconscious and then being enacted. Due to its displacement, this part of the psyche may dictate behaviour from an unconscious position, or it may constellate a compensatory pattern in order to restore balance. The degree to which the expression of these splintered parts is destructive rests on the intensity of the factors leading to the split between good and bad, and the extent to which this endangers the functioning of the psyche. The less there is an inner conflict raging between opposing forces, the more susceptible the individual is to unconscious enactment. The conflict promotes more awareness of both oppositional forces as well as the alchemical transformation that may occur between them. According to this view, evil is a domination of the individual by hateful and destructive complexes within the personality, which tend to take over and possess the perpetrator . According to Stein, a strong influx of archetypal energy and content from the unconscious shades the light of ego consciousness and interferes with a person's ability to make moral distinctions (Stein, 1995). On a collective level, Jung describes this as an "uprush of mass instincts symptomatic of a compensatory move of the unconscious which was possible because the conscious state of the people had become estranged from the natural laws of human existence" (Jung,1946, p. 221). Evil is seen here as an estrangement from our own natures or the natural laws of existence. The necessity of dialoguing with the ancient and primal instincts within us that tend to dominate us unconsciously is important in averting destructive effects (Stein public lecture, April 7, 2006). In bringing attention to them, and engaging with them, we can consciously create another scenario rather than acting them out unknowingly.

Evil is also relative and dependent on a judgment in a given moment. It only really exists when someone makes a judgment that something is evil. When judgments are applied to our own personalities and psychologies we are touching on shadow material, those parts of ourselves we judge, and out of shame or dislike hide away and repress. The school disturber is both suffering from oppression by personal and cultural judgments, as well as the shame and paralysis engendered by futile struggles in the world. In an attempt to satisfy a longing for repletion, or to achieve some superhuman feat, the unconscious influences the instigator to be a messenger for its denied and furious force. The more denied, the more furious it becomes. The more compelled one feels to relegate this type of power to the darkness and to close the lid on it, the more one is faced with outbursts of the kind described earlier in this chapter. As shown, the act of denial begins even in kindergarten where youngsters are guided to hide their natural aggression, rather than to give it useful expression through the forms of fantasy, play, and movement.

Jane Katch (2001) gives a wonderful example of her own struggle when deciding what level of violent play would be acceptable for the five and six year-olds in her class. She describes the following scene in the classroom:

> "Daniel, Seth and Gregory are playing the suicide game. Seth commands Gregory to sit on a chair so that they can blow him up. Seth hands Gregory a plastic apple pretending that he is feeding him and in a loud aside to the other kids says, "its really a hand grenade. Turning to Gregory he says, "Do you know you're gonna explode, Gregory? It's gonna kill you"! Their laughter contrasts sharply with their words, making the scene even more macabre and disturbing to me, but Gregory appears unconcerned. "I'm gonna commit suicide to myself", he chortles. "Eeee"! He explodes happily onto the floor". Can we put on a play of this for the whole class?" he asks me."

After this game, Katch decides that she is going to be like all the other teachers and stop the expression of violent play in the classroom. The children are sad about this and try to negotiate with her around finding an acceptable level of violent play in order for them to have the opportunity to express in this way. In attempting to validate her decision, Katch remembers an exchange she had with her teacher, Bruno Bettelheim, concerning a child in her class with whom she was running out of patience. Bettelheim had intimated that perhaps Katch wanted to do away with this child, not recognizing her own violent reaction to the child. Bettelheim (1975) had said to her, "you must find out, eh? If you want to understand the murderous fantasies of these difficult children, first you must be willing to look at your own" (p. 7). In order to learn empathy for the experience of the children, Katch was being asked to explore her own violent tendencies. Given this awareness of both her own aggressive impulses and those of the children, she questions whether a place could be made in school for understanding these fantasies, instead of shutting them out. She wonders whether she and the children can discover when play of this kind helps learning and self-development in a way that doesn't interfere with schoolwork.

Katch's approach to incorporating the natural aggressive tendencies of the children into the classroom reflects an ability to hold both "good" and "evil" in a container that embraces both. Support for impulses that are usually shunned, will allow shadow material to rise to consciousness and make it applicable to interpersonal interaction in a meaningful way. As Katch suggests, not only does this need to happen among the children. It is also necessary that she herself explore her own tendencies toward aggression in order to better understand and empathize with the children. Using challenging experiences in a way that fosters growth, rather than represses the experience itself, leads to transformation of an existing dynamic. This would be an important step for the individuation process of these children. This would also be an important step for every individual within the school system. In encouraging each person on all levels to become more familiar with his or her own shadow, aggressive, or violent tendencies, more acceptance of these parts could be cultivated, which in turn would allow more openness to explore them.

In bringing these ideas back to the topic of alienation and violence in the school system I would like to refer to the following quote from C.H. Cooley.

> "I do not look upon affection, or anger, or any other particular mode of feeling, as in itself good or bad, social or antisocial, progressive or retrogressive. It seems to me that the essentially good, social or progressive thing, in this regard, is the organization and discipline of all emotions by the aid of reason, in harmony with a developing general life, which is summed up for us in

conscience. That this development of the general life is such as to tend ultimately to do away with hostile feeling altogether is not clear ... that it ought to disappear is certainly not apparent" (Rodkin, Pearl, Farmer & van Acker 2003, p. 73).

Cooley's writings reflect societal views in the 1920s concerning human nature and the social order. Dislike and enmity, along with love, friendship, and kindness were seen as complementary parts of a developing sense of self towards wholeness, while hostility and other expressions of animosity were viewed as normal outgrowths of the individual's participation in society. Society judgmentally favours certain natural human expressions while shunning others as dark and unsavoury. The school bully or shooter embodies the avoided expressions so often repressed by society. The marginalization of these qualities leads to their manifesting in the city shadow as mirrored in disparaged and misunderstood youth.

Summary

In reviewing the above chapter the following points are made.

- The shadow holds aggression, which has been disavowed and culturally repressed. The more a quality is repressed, the more it contributes to shadow material, entrenching the unwanted parts in the unconscious. As with any marginalized quality placed in forbidden darkness, the more it is repressed the more aggression builds into a malevolent force that bursts out in destructive ways. In insisting on expression, the aggressive instincts will make themselves known through outbursts, acts of violence, and destruction.
- When the shadow is not recognized in oneself it is projected on others, and it is then that aggressive or violent tendencies are seen as existing outside of oneself, thus alienating one's true nature from consciousness of the self, and also alienating oneself from others.
- When collective denial of unconscious aggression occurs, individuals holding this quality are scapegoated by the collective and usually cast out from the community in order to rid collective consciousness of the undesirable aggression and violence. This too creates a process of alienation in which collective awareness

is alienated from itself in denying part of its own instinctual nature.

- In a system recognizing the collective shadow, the individual is freed from the role of the identified patient and disturbance can then be consciously addressed on a collective level.
- The individuation process becomes immobilized when longing for an *imago* figure leads to an inability to be effective in one's own life. This may also lead to angry acts of destructiveness.
- In supporting and acknowledging the path of individuation, shadow material can be made useful, meaningful, and creative. Individuation leads to collective relationship through communion with the world at large. The personal is developed to enrich the collective in a process where each informs the other.

The power of the unconscious figure when unacknowledged by the conscious mind may cause havoc and tragedy, for its power grows in proportion to the degree it remains unconscious and unrequited. In most cultures of the world instinctual human aggression is disavowed. When it is acknowledged as part of human nature it is dealt with in a non-shaming way, often through the telling of cultural myths and tales. Although very prevalent in our culture in the more acceptable form of war and violence against others who are seen as threatening to the social or national identity, aggression is not supported in individual experience. As a result aggressive tendencies become a relatively unknown, denied, alienated, and uncomfortable experience closed out of most human interactions, at least consciously. Aggression and violence though do leak out from the unconscious realms in which they reside, often creating surprise, shock, and other reactions on their emergence. In bringing the floodlight of awareness to the internal unconscious violent dramas being played out, not only can the individual find a place to air and transform these, but the social system can learn more about these dynamics, aiding the collective community in learning how to deal with them in a way that is beneficial. An example of how this can be done has been shown through the experience of Derek earlier in this chapter. In terms of school violence, this would mean education on how to harness the meaning of unconscious imperatives so as to foster the growth of the system and everyone within it. This aspect of education is sorely missing from schools, betraying the true goal of education, namely the flowering of each individual in his or her own unique way.

This chapter has used a Jungian lens to explore school disturbance evidenced in the symptomatic behaviour of aggressive youth. In the next chapter experiences of youth within the school system will be looked at through the exploration of image, fairy tale, and myth.

CHAPTER FOUR

Interventive methods

Beyond the rational

In this chapter the worlds of alienation and violence will be popu-
lated with the figures, spirits, and archetypes that exist in realms
that may not usually be held in human awareness. The parallel
worlds or other dimensions in which these figures live out their
myths and engage in their interactions, battles, loves, and deaths
are usually mostly unconscious, but present themselves through
dreams, myths, fairy tales, fables, synchronicities, disturbances,
and symptomatic behaviours. The tools offered by process-oriented dreambody work, techniques of personification, active imagination, dream-telling and analysis, and the use of myth and fairy
tales are extremely effective in penetrating the often-found barriers
and resistances erected by most youth. In particular, the child or
adolescent who is angry and isolated will be strongly defensive
when approached through attempts at relationship. I have found
the use of imaginal methods, which will be further described, to
be helpful in cultivating connection and drawing the individual
out from behind the mask he or she presents to the world. These
techniques are also useful in group work.

Image, myth, and fairy tales

Image

The use of image is well known as a method of accessing unconscious material. The use of image is more familiarly known through methods of dream interpretation where dream figures are explored in order to understand aspects of individual and collective psychology. In addition, there are many other imaginal approaches that are extremely pertinent when working with children and adolescents, particularly in the field of school alienation and violence. The exploration of imaginal figures and forms allows underlying experience to become readily known to conscious awareness. Image is not only a visual phenomenon. It can be experienced in other modalities as well, such as auditorily, emotionally, and through posture or gesture (Hillman, 1975). Visual images, sounds, body experiences, and movements are gateways into the nature of phenomena, which, upon entering and traversing, bring one to an experience of the true nature of the dreaming field.

Mindell (2000) talks of *dreaming* as the essence and intentional field of all phenomena from which images and experiences arise. This dreaming field makes its presence known so that it can be integrated into awareness on a consensus reality level. In order for essence to be embodied it needs to be accessed through images and body experiences, bringing its inherent quality and nature to individual conscious awareness. In accessing the tendencies of the intentional field and making them more known on a conscious level, the path that nature intends is lived more fully.

> "You are not emotionally or physically separable from anything you observe, be it a particle, a tree, or another person. The sense of separateness arises from marginalizing the non-consensus aspects of sensory-grounded perception. Every observation in CR (consensus reality) is based on non-consensual, participatory exchanges in dreaming. From the NCR (non-consensus reality) viewpoint in quantum mechanics, it is no longer clear exactly who is the observer and who is the observed. Both flirt with one another in NCR. You are on safer ground if you say that from the viewpoint of NCR, each so-called human observation consists of a piece of nature looking at herself" (Mindell, 2000, p. 568).

The intentional field may be seen as an entity or energetic field that gives rise to *dreaming*, the constellation of information that presents itself to us in various ways, enlivening our awareness of the dreaming field. *Dreaming* is not a night time occurrence, but occurs all the time, expressing itself through signals that attempt to draw our attention. Image provides a gateway through which *dreaming* emerges in order to be noticed and explored.

The process-oriented dreambody approach

"The dreambody begins with a subtle feeling or sentient experience, which manifests in the body in symptoms and uncontrolled movements, in dreams, in synchronicities, and the like" (Mindell, 2000, p. 509). The dreambody communicates through body symptoms and experiences, dreams, relationship issues, and world events. Mindell gives an example of an individual who had a dream about a hammer, and while telling the dream taps his foot on the floor. In following the tapping of the foot, one follows the dreaming process, just as one might follow an aspect of the night-time dream. In allowing the movement of the foot to guide one, one enters through a "dreamdoor" into another reality or altered experience, in which the meaning of the tapping foot is accessed for the individual through a process of amplification and unfolding of the initial signal. In the tapping of the foot, as with the image of the hammer, may be found a particular quality that the individual needs more of in his life. In entering the dreaming field, one drops one's usual viewpoint in order to get the meaning brought by the dreambody. When integrating this message into everyday consensus reality, one can begin to change one's relationship to oneself, to others, and to the world, enlivening an awareness process that enriches life.

> "The dreambody is your personal, individual experience of the Tao that cannot be said in consensual terms, while dreams and body experiences are like the Tao that can be said. The dreambody is analogous to the quantum wave function in physics. Just as the quantum wave function cannot be seen in consensus reality but can be understood as a tendency for things to happen, the dreambody is a non-consensus reality, sentient,

pre-signal experience manifesting in terms of symptoms and unpredictable motions" (p. 510).

Process-oriented dreambody work provides a methodology by which less identified aspects of individuals, relationships, groups, and systems can be unravelled in order to gain insight into the deeper meaning of what is calling to be discovered. Awareness of these usually unknown or unfamiliar aspects of existence can then be enhanced. In order to embark on this journey, modalities such as vision, audition, proprioception (inner body feeling), and movement are used to enter behind the "dreamdoors". Travelling toward deep sentient experiences allows a re-emergence with new knowledge and awareness. Perceiving the world and its phenomena from a process-oriented, *dreaming* perspective, enables one to access experience at a level beyond what is usually known and identified. Here is an example of how to track emerging *dreaming* through the use of body and form.

> Maria and Carla sit together on the couch each time we meet for group. They seem to mirror each other, neither one saying very much, mostly staring blankly at other group members as we chat together. Initially, they do not engage in group activities, preferring to remain on the couch together. As they become more familiar with the group situation they do begin to contribute a little, although they need encouragement in order to engage.
>
> Their physical appearances are very similar, robust-looking, with rounded forms and glowing verdant skin, reminders of maiden goddesses. I become fascinated with how their facial expressions are so contrary to the atmosphere conjured by the rest of their bodies. Each week, their faces carry a downward turn to mouths, lowered eyes, slight frowns—an almost grumpy configuration in their features, bodies slumped on the couch. In their brief sharing with the group they both identify as being depressed and having relationship difficulties with their families who are over-controlling and oppressive. They had both been having problems in school due to their insolent behaviour and angry outbursts.
>
> One week I bring my instant Polaroid camera to our meeting and offer the following activity to the group. We take photographs of each other as we engage in our usual fashion in the group encounter. Some of the photographs are of group members together, while others are of

single individuals. We then sketch the outlines of shapes and forms that speak to us from the photos of ourselves. Maria and Carla become interested in a photograph that shows them on the couch together. Maria draws the outlines of their bodies as two rounded shapes, huddled together.

The next step of the exercise is to imagine and feel into what it would be like to be that shape, in other words to become the shape, to take on the posture with one's own body, and to notice what that experience is like. What image emerges on becoming the shape, what feeling occurs, and what does this conjure up in one's imagination? Maria's image is of a pair of ripe red apples in the rounded shapes of herself and Carla. I invite her to imagine being the apple and to notice the qualities that the apple embodies. After some minutes of introspection Maria says, "I am so juicy and full of sweetness; there is so much abundance in me! I am so full and round. I want to burst out of my skin and share my juiciness with everyone". And with that she flings out her arms with a huge smile on her face and looks around the group. "Go ahead", I say, "share that juiciness with us." Maria, still smiling, begins to sing, gesturing to other participants to sing with her. She sings and dances, pulling others to their feet, inviting them to join her. The atmosphere in the group has become festive and vital.

Afterwards Maria shares that she has had dreams about musicals in which theatrical stars show off their beauty and talent. She has never realized that inside her lies this juicy and abundant self. She has mainly identified as being oppressed, downtrodden, and miserable. Now her demeanour has changed, and she happily says that she will never forget who she truly is.

In the above experience, Maria was able to utilize an image to dip into a part of herself that was lying beneath her awareness. She had already been dreaming of this aspect, but was not identified with her dream figures. The unconscious nudged her into meeting the qualities held within the image of her rounded form that had flirted with her in the photograph. In exploring this image, the essence of the juicy part of herself emerged to be integrated into her conscious awareness. Prior to this she would not have identified herself as "juicy" or abundant, being alienated from this aspect of her psychology. We could surmise that this alienation was in part connected to her oppressive relationship with family members who did not appreciate her expressive nature. On encountering this new aspect within her and subsequently integrating it into her view of herself, Maria lost her surliness in interaction with peers and teachers alike. After her group experience she often had a smile on her face and brought a joyful presence into subsequent group meetings.

Symptoms and disturbance are often experienced as bringing confusion and chaos. Chaos can be interpreted as the symptomatic, confusing, conflictual, lesser-known aspects of psyche. Both chaos and form can be depicted as co-present lying within image, so that "chaos mothers itself into form, and each form embodies a specific chaos " (Berry, 1982, p. 2). Encountering both chaos and form, necessitates the giving up of traditional linear and literal ways of approaching a work, relying more on an imaginative approach that can also embrace chaos. Working the images, developing our love of their play, being unknowing and fluid, all bring Eros back into the context, enlivening psyche's expression and an expansion of who we know ourselves to be.

Archetypal psychology

Archetypal psychology views the archetype as embodying the imaginal. Image is viewed as an expression of soul. The fantasy images hold the psychological content, and the exploration and deepening of image allows a symptom or presentation to become an experience. An image with its own sensibility and autonomy carries psychological potential for the subject (Hillman 1975). The psyche is seen to be much larger than its personal representation, and as such, embodies the individual while also manifesting through the experience of the individual, using him or her as a vehicle for itself. The basic unit in this process is the image, "a universal, cosmological entity, not subjective and beyond the personal" (p. 48). The psyche is therefore autonomous and self-directed, and creates from itself through the medium of symptoms.

In archetypal psychology, experiences brought by the images present themselves to the individual. Symptoms are therefore psychic manifestations, pieces of psyche, bringing messages of and from the psyche itself. The concept of the symptom and its presentation is taken outside of the personal into the cultural component, viewing images and archetypes as relevant to the collective, as well as to the personal individuation journey. The interconnectedness of the personal and collective aspects of psyche is possible due to the idea of image being a connecting factor between them. Image links the personal with the collective as the archetype brings information and consciousness to both.

In personifying images and representations of psyche, in recognizing them as entities in and of themselves, in experiencing these as other bringing their own wisdom, we save ourselves from the tyranny of egocentricity by freeing the soul from its identity with the ego (Hillman, 1975). This is achieved through the multifold parts and many styles of the fantasy figures and archetypes that present themselves to us. Personifying is a method of knowing through imagining and understanding. Through dreaming into the experience of the image or form, we begin to feel and understand the connectedness between that and one's own mythical reality. Psychological ideas arise from the psyche and return to it reflecting the deepest questions of the soul. We psychologize things by exploring them through fantasy, which involves "seeing into" them and entering their experience. This activity sees through what presents, to find its psychological significance, and connects ideas to their psychic premises in the archetypes (Hillman, 1975). Maria's experience as described above is a good example of how the activities of personifying and psychologizing can be applied, allowing the image to present bits of psyche to awareness for integration into the conscious mind.

Archetypal psychology does not have as its intention the fixing of the symptom. It rather wants to make a relationship with the symptom, and bring into awareness the different parts that are present, particularly those that are unusual, mysterious, or disturbing. As with the process-oriented dreambody approach, the images are hosted and enlivened, allowing the individual to not only gain an understanding of how they exist within him or her, but also how they connect the individual to the larger realm of the collective and universal. In this way more psychic space is developed and suffering is reduced when one is able to step outside of the constriction that comes about from identifying only with the symptom and its resultant discomfort. The realization that one's symptom is not only one's own but is psyche speaking, that chaos is the nature of existence and the human condition, and that symptoms are psyche's language, increases the experiential capacity of the individual and society to embrace and explore these phenomena.

What lies within symptomatic alienation and violence in schools may well have deep meaning for the *zeitgeist* of this age. In exploring the images lying behind and within the alienation and violence of youth, insight may be gained into the attempts of psyche to manifest what is presently beneath the surface of conscious awareness. In addition, a pathway is found leading to the more natural expression of the pent-up energy of repressed archetypes misunderstood by our culture. This will not only allow a broader perspective of human nature to be lived, but will also contribute to the growth of individuation, relieving youth offenders from being the ones to carry the stigma for the culture, and enlivening their own growth process. Understanding more about archetypal forces and the way in which they need to be lived through individual members of a society may also contribute to better understanding of existing global violence.

What needs to be incorporated into current approaches working with school disturbance is a reverence for image as representative of natural expressions emerging from psyche. Developing methods further in order to support the exploration of image within the school context would provide helpful intervention for those distressed or disturbed by alienation, the acting out of aggressive tendencies, and violent outbursts in the school system.

Mythodrama

One method that has been developed in the direction of using image with youth presents a model of working within the school system in Switzerland and Sweden on issues of bullying and violence (Guggenbuhl, 1998). The intervention and violence prevention program introduced in a number of schools in these countries consists of seven steps.

1. Teachers and parents are consulted separately by the intervention team.
2. Parents gather in groups to discuss the situation in the school, and to hear teachers' opinions.
3. The team gains an impression of the school culture and the atmosphere in classrooms, gathering information about each level of the school.

4. The core of the program, which is made up of the mythodrama sessions with the students, is implemented. During these sessions the facilitators reiterate the problem to the students without moral condemnation or distinction between perpetrators, culprits or victims, using a "no blame" approach.

5. A story, legend, myth, or real event, which is carefully selected according to the difficulties of the group within the school environment, is presented to the students, depicting the situation in a concealed way. The story is used to open the minds of the students and may be shocking, provocative, or outrageous.

6. The story is left incomplete and the students are invited to carry it on, fantasizing the end themselves, either individually or in small groups.

7. The fantasized ending of the story is used to bring an expanded perspective on the problem and possible solutions, which are then fed back to teachers and parents in the implementation of changes within the system.

The use of Mythodrama serves to divulge the unconscious or hidden emotions, experiences, and anxieties of the students. It also empowers students to find their own solutions to problems and to contribute these to the system. The facilitator assists in clarifying imaginal conclusions and framing them in a way that can then be applied within the school structure. Teachers and parents are included in these changes as they begin to be instituted within the system.

Positive results in using this method are reported in a quantitative and qualitative study carried out in Switzerland and Sweden evaluating the interventions of Mythodrama made in schools in both those countries (Guggenbuhl, Hersberger, Rom & Bostrom, 2005). In placing emphasis on imaginal methods in working with youth at school, a way to access the deeper wisdom of psyche has been found, which brings new insight into all levels of school functioning. These methods have proved to be useful in enhancing the operation of all levels in the school system. A collaborative approach with children, parents, and teachers in developing solutions for schools in crisis proved to be most effective.

Image and myth are valuable in working with youth as they provide a medium most easily accessible to them. The use of fantasy, imagination, and story-telling, offers a powerful approach with which youth can easily identify. This approach is non-threatening and non-authoritarian, valuing each individual's input and providing an outlet for usually repressed emotions.

Active imagination

In Jung's confrontation with the collective unconscious he discovered a way of using creative fantasy. He later called this method active imagination and used it to guide his journey through unconscious realms (Hannah, 1981). In the practice of active imagination one brings one's attention to the image and engages with it through dialogue and action. One enters into an imaginative encounter with the image from the level of the conscious ego-mind, participating by enacting with the image in its drama, spinning out its story in one's imagination (Hannah, 1981). The image-symbols of the unconscious find their way to the level of consciousness through imagination.

> "A conduit that runs from the unconscious to the conscious mind that has the power to convert the invisible forms of the unconscious and make them perceptible to the conscious mind. Imagination is an organ of coherent communication, employing a highly refined, complex language. When we learn to watch it we discover that the imagination is a veritable stream of energy and meaningful imagery; the dream world flowing through us while we are awake. Just as with dreams, the symbolic meanings of the images may be understood by actively engaging with them through active imagination" (p. 21).

As one embarks on the journey through the practice of active imagination, one may meet parts of the psyche that are admired, disliked or disagreeable, and in meeting them, consciousness is broadened to incorporate features of the self hitherto unknown, marginalized or projected. Active imagination is about being able to tolerate the tension between the opposites, and if possible, uniting them in oneself. Not only is it about seeing the images of the unconscious, or actively dealing with them through fantasy, it is also about finding the place and purpose of the processed images in outer life, namely the application of their meaning to ongoing existence as an obligation that each individual carries. Failure to recognize and explore the images of the unconscious leads to painful fragmentation of one's own being. It is this conscious participation that cultivates the active component within the imaginative play.

> "The coming together of conscious mind and unconscious mind on the common ground of the imaginal plane gives us an opportunity to break down some of the barriers that separate the ego from the unconscious, to set up a genuine flow of communication between the two levels of psyche, to resolve some of our neurotic conflicts with the unconscious, and thus to learn more about who we are as individuals" (Johnson, 1986, p. 20).

Dipping into the imagination in this way brings about change in very deep ways, realigning one's attitude and approach to life situations, and enabling one to integrate previously unknown parts of oneself into everyday existence. This process expands awareness, enriching all levels of psyche and personal identity. Active imagination can be used with dream fragments or images, fantasy figures, and people or situations that present to one in actual life. It involves the playing out of imaginal interactions through dialogue and image.

> *Monica has been raised in a very strict home, where her every deed and social interaction is monitored closely by both her parents. Monica has been referred to the special school program as her academic performance has declined—in the previous year she failed every subject—and she has been openly talking of self-destructive acts and suicide. As she speaks in group sessions, I notice that she is quite bitter about life. Not only is she extremely self-hating, she is also disparaging of others and their belief systems.*
>
> *After Monica has spent some weeks in the group and is beginning to get more familiar and comfortable with us, she shares that she goes to bed each night with a machete under her pillow. She has fears of somebody coming into her room to attack her and wants to be prepared "just in case". When asked who this attacker might be, she replies that she has no idea, but has a gnawing dread that this threat will eventuate. I ask if she would be willing to explore her fear and when she agrees, I invite her to form an image of herself in bed, the machete under her pillow, and the threatening figure entering the room. I assure her that I am there to support her if needed. I coach her*

to engage with the figure and to begin dialoguing with it. Here is an extract from her work.

Figure:	*You've been a bad girl and I'm here to make sure that you behave yourself. I've come to punish you in the worst way. You have no idea how brutal I can be!*
Monica:	*(Shivering in fear). Go away—get out. I hate you!*
Figure:	*I'm never leaving. You are going to do as I say, otherwise you will pay the price. You have had inappropriate thoughts and shown bad behaviour. You're disgusting! I'm going to make sure you never do that again. (The figure steps into the room menacingly).*
Monica:	*I'm so afraid of you. You paralyze me. I feel as though you have a hold over me that I just can't break. You have so much power. I wish you would leave me alone. I want to be free of you. (She sobs).*
Figure:	*(Coming closer). Yes, I am so powerful—you have no idea. I can tear you limb from limb, dismember you, feed you to the wild beasts. You will never know the full extent of my power.*
Monica:	*I need power. Teach me about power. I want to know how to be powerful. You can teach me. I will be your student.*
Figure:	*I am not here to teach. I am here to punish. You are my victim. (The figure advances further into the room nearing the bed on which Monica lies).*
Monica:	*(Freeing herself from her frozen fear state, reaches for the machete. With a blood-curdling scream she launches herself at the figure, slashing with the machete again and again. The figure lies dying on the floor). Now, who is powerful? I have got you and you are in my power. You will never trouble me again. I have beaten you. I am the powerful one!*

As Monica completes this active imagination she stands up and in a victory pose she flexes her muscles, showing her strength, a huge grin on her face.

In subsequent weeks Monica reports to the group that she is feeling a lot stronger in herself. She has been able to stand up to her parents a couple of time and assert herself more in her relationships. She is no longer having suicidal thoughts.

This composite case example clearly illustrates the effectiveness of using imagination in an active way to enter presenting images in order to engage with them. This engagement helps to support unknown parts of the identity that lie beneath consciousness. In Monica's case, she had little connection with her own strength or volition, having succumbed to the image of herself as "less than". She had turned against herself, hating who she was, and giving up on her life, her life force subdued by her self-criticism and bitterness toward others. In entering the images that kept her awake at night, she managed to access and unfold qualities that had previously been beyond her reach, enriching her identity and empowering her in her life. The image of the persecutor that appeared to her embodied her parents' hypervigilance and denigration of her, which internalized became her own self-hatred. Through the medium of active imagination she was able to deal with the complex in an imaginal way, rather than address it rationally, to which she had been resistant. Accessing this unidentified part of herself through active imagination freed her from its hold over her. It offered her a powerful way to connect with the hidden and denied aspects of her true self.

Active imagination becomes a valuable tool for those who are able to apply its techniques. The use of image and story assist individuals in contacting unavailable aspects of their unconscious selves, bringing this material to consciousness. The creative aspect of active imagination appeals to youth, and is helpful in breaking through their usual resistance to reveal themselves. For suffering and victimized school students, the unravelling of the images appearing to them not only helps them to contact their emotional reactions and express them in some way, but also brings them to a deeper understanding of their own natures. The bridge between the known and unknown parts of themselves, created through the technique of active imagination, allows them to journey between the divided parts of themselves and to gain access to formerly alienated collective spirits dwelling within them. Breaking through their alienation from these aspects of themselves, opening passages into them, allows recognition of parts perhaps projected on others, but certainly marginalized in themselves, thus reducing the spell of alienation suffered. It is then that something new emerges in the self-identity, which can be made useful in outer existence, as in Monica's case where she felt more powerful and able to engage with her parents using her newly found strength.

Dreams

The images of dreams present themselves to awareness in symbolic form. Much has been written about dreams. For Freud and Jung, dreams and their images were gateways to the unconscious, dream analysis forming the foundation of their approaches. Indigenous tribes also utilize dreams to understand what lies beyond their known worlds, some seeing dreams as the messages of their gods (Kaplan Williams, 1977). Although going more deeply into the origins and methods of working with dreams is beyond the scope of this book, I do highlight one aspect of dream work as a useful intervention in entering beyond the defenses erected by troubled youth. The telling of dreams offers a very useful method in working with children and adolescents who seem to have a natural interest in this topic, stimulating lively interaction both individually and in groups.

> *In beginning sessions I am having an ongoing struggle in making connection with the troubled young people who have been referred to me for either individual or group therapy. My attempts to make conversation, express my feelings, be friendly, defer to them, invite them to speak, find out more about what lies beneath the hostility and silence, support their experience, be confronting, and so on, all fall flat. My suggestions for art, games, exercises or sharing receive blank stares, snide comments, or silence. Some are shy and reserved, others hostile and defiant. I ponder about how I am going to reach them.*
>
> *After trying for a number of weeks to get our work together off the ground, I decide to use dreams as an access into relationship. Without much talk or explanation, at the start of our next group session I invite group members to take a piece of paper and draw a dream that they remember. I emphasize that this need not be a work of art, that even an abstract representation would suffice, and that they need not show their drawings or share their dreams if unwilling to do so. To my surprise, my suggestion is taken up with some enthusiasm. For the next half hour there is a hum of engagement in the room as each person takes paper and crayons and busily immerses him or herself in the drawing. When completed, group members begin to chat with each other sharing their pictures and dreams. I invite individuals to share these in the group, which many do with excitement. Through the sharing of dream images and stories a new*

connection is formed among us. This experience creates a gateway into further deepening of relationship, cultivating a sense of belonging in future group meetings.

Dream images provide a language so fascinating that few can resist their compelling nature. Once we enter the realm of the dream, the symbolic material pulls us into a parallel existence in which mythical elements speak to us, opening consciousness into different realities. The symbolic content of dreams has significance. Even if kids are unwilling to go into the symbolism, the telling of the dream itself creates it's own numinous field in which the images of psyche manifest. According to Jung dream symbols act as a bridge from the unconscious to consciousness transcending the opposition by bridging the two. The symbols create the bridge leading from the inexpressible to the conscious mind.

> "The dream is a little hidden door in the most secret and hidden recesses of the soul, opening into that cosmic night which was psyche long before there was any ego-consciousness, and which will remain psyche no matter how far out ego-consciousness extends. For all ego-consciousness is isolated; because it separates and discriminates, it knows only particulars, and it sees only those that can be related to the ego. All consciousness separates; but in dreams we put on the likeness of that more universal, truer, more eternal man dwelling in the darkness of primordial night. There he is still the whole, and the whole is in him, indistinguishable from nature and bare of all egohood. It is from these all-uniting depths that the dream arises, emphasizing our blood kinship with all of mankind" (Jung, 1946, p. 145–147).

Dreams reflect motifs comparable to the motifs of mythology. All dream images are important in themselves, reflecting psychological situations and having a special significance of their own. The symbol in the dream has the value of a parable as it teaches about pieces of psyche and their dynamics. True symbols are expressions of a content not yet consciously recognized or conceptually formulated, but offering an entry into the unknown meaning behind the symbol (Jung, 1946). It is important to consider the meaning of the symbol in relation to the conscious situation and psychological state of the dreamer. These symbols can then later be linked to archetypes, reflecting collective material. Once the collective aspect emerges, the link between individuals becomes more apparent dispelling the isolation experienced by the lone ego-consciousness. The numinous quality of dreams provides a connecting factor among people as a deep experience is shared even though it may be beyond words. It is then that the individual's own story can be located in the larger story of humanity. The *numinosum* is spoken of by Jung as an external, objective, divine cause, a quality that belongs to a visible object or the influence of an invisible presence causing a peculiar alteration of consciousness (Storr, 1983).

Focusing on the dreams of group participants, and sharing the stories of these dreams within the group situation, helps break through the resistance set up by participants. Dreams offer a rich way of exploring identity and finding out more about oneself. The use of dreams facilitates the sharing of psychic material usually held secret, creating more intimacy between participants. The sense of connectedness among group members dispels experiences of alienation allowing recognition of the human condition shared by those present. The exploration of dreams brings an experience of the numinous. Entering the numinous in a group experience leads to strong bonding of group participants. The experience of somebody else as "other", of whom one needs to be wary, falls away as the sharing of images from dream realms brings a recognition of "other" as self. This experience of belonging and connection is of the utmost importance in working with adolescent alienation and violence. This will be further explored in the next chapter.

Myth and fairy tales

In exploring violence and its mythical components, how to better support a violent event through recovery of the mythic will be illustrated below. Myths and fairy tales offer insights into psychological dynamics that present themselves during the course of life. Both myths and fairy tales offer models for human behaviour that give meaning and value to life (Bettelheim, 1975). Like dreams, myths and fairy tales speak in the language of symbols representing unconscious content and inner psychological phenomena in symbolic form. They appeal to both the conscious and unconscious aspects of mind and to the need for ego-ideals. The figures and events found within mythical stories are archetypal, reflecting psychological aspects that promote higher states of selfhood. Events found within myths are grandiose, awe-inspiring, addressing superhuman challenges and feats, whereas fairy tales bring themes concerning life patterns and events in the every day lives of the story's figures. Responding to myths and fairy tales brings forth emotional content stirring repressed or forgotten feelings within the listener. Previously unconscious or lost material may then enter one's awareness and become accessible for processing.

More can be learned from fairy tales than from any other type of story about the inner problems of human beings and of the right solutions to their predicaments in any society (Bettelheim, 1975). Fairy tales speak to all levels of the human personality by portraying the human dilemma through the images held within the tale and by their interaction with each other. Fairy tales offer new dimensions to imagination, allowing unconscious material to be revealed through the contents of the tale. Within the myth or tale, good and evil are equally represented as portrayed by the figures of the story. Evil is not disavowed, and in meeting the evil witch or destructive giant, the reader is exposed to both the alluring, powerful aspects of the evil one as well as the destructive havoc that it can generate. Most fairy tales illustrate clearly how evil is overcome by good, providing a container for the playing out of the struggle between these forces, whereas myths generally do not have happy endings and represent the ongoing saga of life. Giving credence to these powerful stories validates the internal and external ways in which these dynamics play out for individuals and societies.

Ares

In exploring aggressive and violent events, a number of aspects of the god Ares may assist in bringing greater understanding of the meaning of these events. The violence of Ares can be seen as sacred, found in the altered states that take over when one is seized by fury. Ares presents himself through action, rage, and brutal power and it can be assumed that in the background of any violent or aggressive act lies the god Ares, the act being a sacrament to him (Hillman, 2004). Ares is "the divinity who rages, strikes death, stirs panic, driving individual humans mad and collective societies blind" (Hillman, 2004, p. 42). Ares appears to be the most disliked of all the gods inspiring little real devotion or affection. This force, this god-like power represented in the archetypal image of Ares, so prevalent in human behaviour through recorded history in acts of violence and war, is deemed inhuman and relegated to the realms of the unconscious through dislike of him. Ares though is also an ancient god of agriculture, Mother Earth demanding violence and bloodshed in order to promulgate the new from her chthonic depths. Could it possibly be that the essence of violence gives rise to reformulation and rebirth and that the expression of aggression or violence is a needed dynamic on a collective level in order for something else to grow? "All great works of art find their full force in those moments when the conventions of the world are stripped away and our weaknesses, vulnerability and mortality are confronted" (Hedges, 2002, p. 91). Violence and its expression may create the impulse for creativity itself.

The Germanic god Wotan also represents this archetypal duality. He is described as both the god of storm and lord of the dead, and as the master of secret knowledge and god of the poets (Ninck, 1936). Wotan is not only a god of rage and frenzy, but intuitive and inspiring. Wotan is aligned with Hermes and his ability to work magic, a nature spirit who "returned to life in the figure of Merlin of the Grail legend and who became, as the *spiritus Mercurialis*, the sought-after arcanum of the alchemists" (Jung, 1961, p. 313).

In addition to being viewed as both creative and destructive as can be seen in the explication of the figures of Ares and Wotan, violence is also recognized as a means of cultivating love and connection. "When faced with violence and its horrors, love binds those sharing the awful (awe-full) experience in a potent way" (Hillman, 2004, p. 142). The ancient Greeks linked acts of violence with love, and indeed it was Aphrodite, the goddess of love, who became the mistress of Ares, the god of war. Aphrodite, the wife of the ironsmith Hephaistos, takes Ares as her lover and as the two lie together Hephaistos casts a net of chain over them imprisoning them. In those moments the two are inseparable (Homer trans, 1968). The attraction that brought them together is the inevitable striving for wholeness and balance, each compensating the other in areas where there is a gap. Their union, represents the coming together of complementary forces, a *hieros gamos*, a sacred union, the final *coniunctio*, the marriage of the opposites, a state of perfect balance and harmony sought after by many spiritual traditions.

Indeed, there are many stories of how love bonds are formed by those experiencing violence. After the Columbine High School shootings, members of the community reported experiencing a bonding and connection with each other never known before. The experience of closeness among this community's members appears to have been sustained over time. When the Red Lake shooting occurred, members of Columbine High School visited Red Lake School to share their experiences and to be a support for the Red Lake community, creating a bond of compassion and love through their shared experience (Rury, 2005). This is noticed too in the close bond that forms between soldiers on the battlefield when surrounded by scenes of violence and horror. Recognition that violence leads to love and connection, and that love and human connectedness are rarely viewed as a priority in our culture, cultivates a new way of honouring these qualities and of supporting their emergence and development. Learning about these factors as part of a school's curriculum would be a wonderful addition to the syllabus.

Not only does violence lead to appreciation of caring and friendship, it also connects one with a higher spiritual meaning, binding those sharing the experience to each other. Violence provides a shared sense of meaning or cause arising from the communal experience within the violent context. It is almost as if the surrender to a force greater than oneself constellates an experience so intense it is analogous to some kind of deep spiritual encounter (Hedges, 2002). In this context violence can be seen as a needed natural force, cultivating new creativity and connection in its aftermath.

In examining the role that myths and fairy tales play in the field of school alienation and violence, it becomes apparent that within these stories a place is made for violence and aggression in which they are acknowledged as part of human nature. Indeed these qualities are seen as necessary forces in ensuring that both good and evil are encountered amidst the panoply of human possibilities. Without the opportunity to grapple with these parts within one's own nature, one may never be able to reconcile the challenges of life as incentives for the growth of self and psyche. If education included awareness of these dynamics, and children were guided and encouraged to deal with these forces both within themselves and within others, repression of these factors would be much diminished. Destructive forces could be disarmed and their essential qualities utilized in creative, loving, and meaningful ways. Without this process occurring it is no wonder that destructive impulses explode unexpectedly to create chaos and devastation within the school environment. Embracing the qualities that exist within the range of human experience through processes of honing and cultivation, engenders a sense of acknowledgement and acceptance of them. This in turn leads to the feeling that one belongs among others of one's kind. Connection is formed through the exchange of common experiences and shared humanity. A place is made for each individual within the web of human belonging. This would certainly apply to the school-going child who, on encountering his or her own aggressive impulses and expressions, would be guided to deal with them in a supportive way, thus fostering a sense of belonging to a larger system able to contain all of one's expression. This attitude would also embody the loving and creative aspects that ultimately emerge as a result of expressed violence and if developed in good time, might obviate the need for violent action. In order to illustrate these ideas I wish to share with you a story told by Clarissa Pinkola Estes beautifully describing the struggle against evil and its relegation to a place of safety (Pinkola-Estes, 1990).

Mother moon

Here is the story of the Stolen Mother Moon who is captured by the evil marsh dwellers living outside of a village. The evil ones push her down into the marsh and roll a huge boulder on top of her so that her light cannot shine forth. In the absence of Mother Moon's light, the evil ones are able to flourish. The villagers are no longer able to leave the village due to the evil presence outside of the village and fall into loss, suffering, and despair, beset by the presence of the dark evil. At last the villagers unable to keep going, decide that they need to go and look for the Moon Mother and they set out into the bog to search her out, carrying torches to light their way. Eventually one night after searching for a long time and in fear of their lives, they find the huge boulder with a lip of light shining from around its rim and manage to roll it back. As they do so, the most beautiful light they had ever seen shines forth from the face of Mother Moon. Mother Moon, freed, climbs back into the sky where she once again shines forth on most nights. The nights when she veils herself people have learned to stay by the hearth, where the light of the fire keeps them safe, until she reveals herself once again, in order to guide them through the bog.

Pinkola-Estes (1990) finds the following meaning in the tale. It can be seen that the village moves from paradise to upheaval and danger, representing the spiritual journey moving us from the paradise of infancy into encounter with the darker aspects of human nature that both threaten survival and provide opportunities for individuation. As the paradisiacal aspects are banished, fear and defensiveness develop in reaction to forces outside of oneself perceived as threatening to one's wellbeing. These usually come about through lack of love and acknowledgement. The evil ones particularly represent those darkest thoughts that flourish where there is no light, where there is an absence of love. The Mother Moon loves human beings while the evil ones hate the human heart.

With the presence of Mother Moon and the love and light that she brings, one is able to do the work that pulls one once again from the depths of despair. This work may take the form of grappling with internal dynamics that lead to a loss of self-acknowledgement, or to confrontation with the forces that create separation and alienation within the social or community context. Needs for wholeness, harmony, and relationship search out the light. Loss and alienation are dispelled when the light can once again share its illumination. When light is freed to reveal the previously unseen, one can find the sublime in the ridiculous, beauty in the disavowed, and meaning in disturbance. In the school situation, falling into despair at the hands of the evil ones can be aligned to being at the mercy of other adults and children who may hit, taunt, or hurt us, expect the impossible from us, or fail to recognize our own light. The dark places in the psyche depict the humiliation, shame, abuse, name-calling, and disregard that create a fright, flight, or fight reaction in the child, resulting in introjected self-hatred and despair as the evil ones within then take over. Once someone has been misused, all kinds of evil thoughts are introjected into the individual psyche resulting in the loss of the light and the dark night of the soul.

Another level of the tale reminds us of the importance of community. Mother Moon needs the joint effort of the villagers in order to be freed. It is a communal quest that leads to her liberation once again and hence to the survival of the village community. This beautifully illustrates how important others are in order to bring about individual growth. One always needs a community to watch one's back no matter how much personal work one does on oneself (Moore, 1989). Community allows transformation to occur that may not be possible as a lone individual. In community effort, not only is the individual protected, but the community also receives the gift of illumination.

With the absence of quality time spent between parents and children, the sharing of stories, myths, and tales has mostly fallen away in Western society. Youth then turn to TV and videogames for mythical roots and meaning. Here mighty battles are fought between good and evil forces replicating the stories previously accessible through myths and fairy tales. Despite the mythical content of violent shows and games that fill the gap left by the absence of storytelling, many studies have shown that media violence has a detrimental influence on children and youth increasing levels of aggression and disruptive behaviour (Moore et al. 2003). I mention this here as being relevant to the topic of violence of youth, while exploring this theme further is outside the focus of this book. Similarly, access to guns has become prohibitively easy for youth, exacerbating violent encounters. Before the installation of metal detectors at schools, nearly every male youth carried a gun to school in certain neighbourhoods. This too is a vast topic that cannot be covered here. What can be drawn attention to here is the degree to which both media and gun violence have become part of the mythology of our youth today, giving more license for the expression of aggression in destructive ways. From an archetypal perspective, this may open the gateway for the collective shadow and provide a means for it to express itself. Those through whom the shadow speaks have their own reasons and propensity for expression of aggression thus becoming messengers for the archetypal force. Children who have suffered their own tortures and can find no surcease in their environments, spew out their pain and hatred on others as a violent outpouring of the furious Wotan. This becomes their identity in the eyes of the society, at which point they become the demons. However, rather than viewing these children as demonic, they may be seen as harbingers of insight for society, bringing to awareness the forces so necessary for survival which, if consciously encountered, rather than creating destruction and mayhem, may bring empowerment and growth. Constructive guidance is needed in order to support the useful expression of aggressive energy, rather than the demonization of the city shadows who express these archetypal forces for the collective. The earlier that this can begin in childhood, the more the child becomes a model for the society in which he or she lives, demonstrating the teleological purposes of dynamics associated with aggression, mostly avoided or shunned in a society that places so much emphasis on being appropriately "nice" and "good". In this way the light of Mother Moon is then freed to shed its illumination, connecting individuals and community in the web of humanity.

Belonging and connection

> "One has not much noticed that this cold orphan, whose indifference can become criminal, is a fanatic of absence. He is a devotee of solitude, even in the midst of a crowd, because he is faithful to a shadow: bewitching secret, paternal ideal, inaccessible ambition" (Kristeva, 1991, p. 104).

How poignantly these few lines depict the existential dilemma of the individual who lives in isolation—a foreigner cast out of an established social order, mirroring the secrecy of shadow material. Teens who show an absence of hope for the future reflect their despair at not being able to make an impact on their lives and environments. The absence of hope and the despair are linked then with the appeal to some kids of "dark and fascistic imagery and ideology". In fantasizing about ways of expressing their frowned on violent tendencies, they find a sense of meaning and connection that they have not been able to access in other ways. Having been relegated to the fringes of social groups, receiving little or no acknowledgement from their families and from the culture as a whole, connection becomes an imperative for them (Shapiro, 2005). In looking at the shooting incident at Columbine High School, it is not surprising that these powerful images, which are easily available on television and through the Internet, speak to the isolation and rage held by youth. Shadow material that has been repressed and disavowed due to belief systems held within the family and culture, imbues itself in the fantasy life of these youth. From their state of isolation, in receiving ridicule, marginalization, lack of inclusion, and sometimes violence, these youth begin to identify this behaviour, in a twisted way, with connection and community.

On tracing this dynamic back to the aspect of Ares that speaks to love and connection, one can see how violent image and expression may appeal to alienated youth who are regularly exposed to a new mythology of aggression and violence through the images offered to them on a daily basis. Alienated from themselves and from those around them, they turn to the mythical images best offering them connection with their own rageful fantasies. Violent images of horror provide a sense of belonging for them, reflecting their own identification with the rageful parts of themselves as mirrored in the violent enactments on the TV screen.

Ron Taffel (1999) depicts alienation experienced in children as a direct effect of the lack of real time and attention that parents give to kids. "We cannot always tell the ways in which our kids are uniquely different because we just do not spend enough direct one-on-one time with them. The hard truth is that many parents may love their children, but they do not create the time to pay attention to them. They do not really hear them. They do not really see them" (p. 94). Even though hours may be spent together in the home, parents hardly engage with their children without being distracted by something else like the telephone, e-mails, business commitments, and so on. The absence of family connection is linked to the solitude that many children and adolescents report as being present in their lives. Taffel observes kids becoming angry or disheartened at not being clearly seen, yearning for what they are not getting. As a reaction to not being acknowledged or heard, children tend to become withdrawn, believing that what they are trying to express is insufficient to warrant attention. In response, the mass media culture takes the place of what is missed. The anonymity that many children feel is fostered by celebrity-focused mass media, lack of parental individual guidance, and lack of appreciation for the child as a unique idiosyncratic individual. Images and fantasies offered on the television screen replace real relationships. As most children are unable to talk to their parents and other adults about what really matters to them, the stories and images they encounter in television replicate relationship patterns that no longer exist for them within the family. The ability to express imaginatively falls away with a resultant lack of creativity, leading to an inability to problem-solve and difficulty in staying away from risky behaviour. Lack of expressiveness may be linked also to the failure of adults to recognize a child's particular style of expression in the expectation of something more "correct". All of this fosters an increasing sense of alienation among most youth. One can truly wonder about the kinds of images that replace human relatedness. In looking at what is shown on television, there should be no surprise that perfect-looking men and women who engage with each other violently, now become the model images for most youth. The heartfulness of being human becomes lost in the slickness of the world kids enter on a daily basis, surrendering their true vitality to television personae.

School climate is shown to be important too in cultivating student attitudes and behaviours. There is a surprising number of students who experience stress and alienation at school which is directly linked to the most favoured punishments being "unbelonging" interventions (Seita & Brendtro, 2003, p. 58). Humiliation from school staff is also often involved. Violent patterns are found most often among alienated students in negative climates where educators view students as adversaries. In this climate high levels of verbal assault and frequent put-downs of students are encountered in the classroom. A positive school climate invites collaboration from students who are treated fairly and respectfully, where rules are fair and beneficial. In a positive climate where students feel that they belong and are valued, they tend to both contribute more to the system and also flourish more in their own daily lives.

On the other hand, in schools where students receive no inspirational guidance or emotional support, and collaboration is lacking, collective trauma is described as a blow to the basic tissues of social life that damages the bonds attaching people together and that impairs the prevailing sense of communality. Where the spirit of community does not exist as an effective support, an important part of the self disappears. The "we" as a connected entity in a larger communal body is not present (Hull, 2003).

In light of the above it becomes apparent that when containment is lacking for certain emotions frowned on by the culture, the individual child or adolescent seeks a replacement through the medium of the images encountered in everyday life. Many of the images presented are aggressive and violent and these are the ones that seem to constellate a new mythology for those suffering alienation. A new world is created in which the isolated child can feel connected to the images, albeit they are destructive ones. Having no home to shelter strong feelings of anger, disappointment, and hopelessness, the alienated child turns to another realm that mirrors something of his or her own inner world. This fantasy world often provides a model for how to vent unexpressed emotions. When desperation gets too great, this identification with a new mythology of violence, is expelled through hostile and violent acts on those who are perceived as contributing to the pain experienced.

Summary

This chapter has explored alienation and violence through the use of image, myth, and fairy tale. In delving into the symbolic representation of individual and collective experiences of alienated and violent tendencies, insight into these experiences is enlivened and deepened. In attending to, and unfolding symbolic images, awareness of what is held within the image is stimulated. How this is mirrored in psyche is also highlighted. The following ideas have been expressed.

- Image and myth are modalities of exploration that appeal to youth and are more easily accessible to them, constellating less of a threat to them and thus encountering less resistance from them.
- In entertaining images, and in psychologizing or personifying the content of the image, knowledge of lesser-known aspects of the self emerges.
- Embracing image and unravelling it provides an outlet for expressions, either harmonious or disturbing, supported or disavowed. Image acts as a conduit for the expression of previously repressed material, or behaviour disallowed by the social fabric.
- Numinosity experienced through a shared encounter acts as a connecting factor, bringing individuals together in the cultivation of a sense of belonging.

- Violence, besides being destructive, is also useful as a creative force, binding people together through love and caring.
- Myth and fairy tales encourage both inner growth as well as an appreciation for community and social endeavours, cultivating awareness of the human dilemma and it's deeper meaning.
- A new mythology of violence is created when no vessel is provided within the family or cultural context for the containment of disavowed emotions.

In this chapter there have been two main areas of exploration. The application of the allegorical nature of myth and fairy tales to dynamics of alienation and violence among youth has been shown to be useful. Archetypal or mythical figures offer insight into the dual nature of human experience, thus awakening insight into the deeper meaning of existence both individually and universally. Ways in which to apply the use of image in working with disturbed youth have been clarified. Methods found in process-oriented approaches, active imagination, and the use of dreams, have been shown to be helpful in reducing resistance and in facilitating entry into deeper feelings and views. The outcome of such methods has led to revelation of parts of the self previously disregarded or unknown, enhancing the individual's knowledge of herself and improving interaction with others. Tools mentioned in this chapter offer effective methods of encountering youth who show behaviour problems.

CHAPTER FIVE

Preventive measures

Psychodynamic perspectives

Another way of exploring alienation and violence in schools is through an approach that views symptomatic behaviour in light of the unconscious conflicts, deficits, and distortions of intrapsychic structures and internal object relations. The individual's internal world is given paramount importance and is explored through dreams, associations, impulses, wishes, self-images, perceptions of, and psychological reactions to others, and projections heaped upon them.

Exploring psychodynamic phenomena in the arena of alienation and violence among youth can lead to a better understanding of what may be occurring within psychological structures of the potential school offender, allowing us to make better contact with her through empathic understanding. In recognizing these intrapsychic dynamics, early recognition can occur of children with tendencies for violent expression, facilitating remedial action at an early stage. A deeper understanding of what occurs on psychological levels within a child perpetrator of acts of violence can facilitate interaction with him by providing a means to access the authentic split-off parts of the child. In delving into particular patterns observed in experiences associated with anger, aggression, withdrawal, suicidality, self-destructiveness, and violent impulses toward others, not only can we be of help to the disturbed child, but recognizing these patterns can also help us to identify other children who have a tendency toward the same behaviour. In understanding the deeper layers of psychodynamic functioning within the individual, we become more able to understand and acknowledge associated experiences, thus becoming more able to be of help to the child in his loss, pain, or inner conflict.

The ideas which are incorporated in this chapter have been chosen for their relevance to the topic and for their insight into the psychodynamic factors most applicable to the internal experiences of alienated and violent youth in modern society. In this chapter intrapsychic experiences will either be presented clustered into subcategories for the sake of clarity, or be introduced on their own. These may seem to be artificial delineations and are in no way meant to portray that each quality stands on its own without being interconnected with others in the woven fabric of the psychodynamic field. However, this method seems to be the most efficient lending itself to a more in-depth study of each psychological phenomenon as it contributes to the withdrawn states of alienation and to the disturbed expressions of violence.

Deprivation and antisocial tendencies

Winnicott (1984) emphasizes one kind of psychological classification, which he views as vitally important within the framework of the education system. The deprived or relatively deprived child who reveals psychological and behavioural reactions to the deprivation experience needs recognition and support from her environment. Winnicott describes the process of deprivation as follows. "At some point in life the child receives good enough provision from the environment resulting in a continuity of personal being, and then becomes deprived of this. Henceforth the world must be made to acknowledge and repair the injury" (p. 212). The child's unconscious attempts to bring this about result in an antisocial tendency or maladjustment. What was originally occupied by play in the personality now becomes acting out. The resulting clinical

picture can be observed in some kind of destructive behaviour that
attempts to bring back the original framework that has been lost.
The antisocial tendency is characterized by the unconscious drives
of the individual compelling someone to pay attention to the loss.
It implies a period in which there is hope that the restoration of the
lost phenomenon will occur. Even though society may suffer from
the disturbing behaviour, it is important that it be attended to and
contained, because the hope may easily wither and waste away due
to intolerance or mismanagement. When there is hope, instinctual
life becomes active and the individual can use these instinctual
urges, which may include aggressive ones, to make good what has
been hurt. Unfortunately, society is generally not willing to see anything positive in the antisocial activity due to the annoyance at the
disruption, and there is a lack of awareness of how important this
expression really is. Winnicott's emphasis on providing support and
understanding for the disturbing behavioural patterns of youth is
extremely important in approaching alienated and violent youth. It
provides a framework in which to address and deal with disruptive
expression or withdrawn states.

James Grotstein (personal communication, January 27, 2007)
speaks of *conatus,* from the Latin *conatio,* as the principle that guar-
antees the continuity of the self during change. If *conatus* is lacking,
if the degree of elasticity within the self is insufficient to contain the
stress, adaptive change cannot occur and the individual is thrown
into a state of extreme fear, resulting in a psychic retreat and disconnection within the self. As a result of the terror and the scarring
that occurs, a split is created in which the self becomes encapsu-
lated and lost. On experience becoming too painful, this encapsu-
lated part of the self enters a purgatory in which no connection is
possible with the true self thus avoiding distressing feelings. The
healthy part of the self pulls away leaving its stranded twin behind,
who can only communicate through acting out and creating disturbance. In this split position, one finds a huge protest at being born
within which is an unconscious demand for an apology for being
born into such an inhospitable world so filled with suffering. In an
autochthonous mindset the individual imagines that the suffering
that takes place is a result of what he or she has done, unconsciously
deciding that he or she is the cause of everything, the pain of this
belief becoming intolerable and further promulgating withdrawal

into the psychic retreat. Grotstein describes this as the soul being in hock to some devilish force to which the individual surrenders. This psychic retreat projects into the world everything that is bad about itself. The individual becomes cut off from the idea of hope and has to "die" in order to stay alive.

This view suggests that rather than castigating and marginalizing school offenders, their behaviour could be seen as a manifestation of their hope, the hope that somebody might attend to the true self that is suffering and lost. If attention could be given to their authentic experience, these youth might be given a chance to find understanding for the internalized hatred, envy, and revenge that they experience. In finding a context in which to give these most difficult emotions some expression, there is a chance that a process of transformation can occur. There are many lessons in this approach for all levels of the school system. If potentially destructive behaviour is caught early enough, intervening in a supportive and exploratory way may also act as a preventive measure of future eruptions of violence.

In light of the above, aggression and its expression can be seen as a natural stage in the developmental process. Here it needs to be understood as the infant's attempt to engage with its environment and to differentiate the self from what is not the self. The opportunity to hate and be destructive while being contained becomes an achievement in learning to manage the world in a way that can become a positive experience. Aggressiveness is mostly a dramatization of an almost intolerable inner reality. It is a way in which the child makes an attempt to bring his or her inner reality, too terrible to be acknowledged, into relation with external reality (Winnicott, 1984). The individual is challenged to find safe ways of disposing of "badness", and society is similarly challenged in being able to accept these outpourings. Fear-driven aggression can be contained and supported in its expression by providing appropriate management through dramatization in a way that is not dangerous to either the individual or those around him.

> "When children see their own controlled (repressed) aggressive impulses in the aggression of others, this can develop in an unhealthy way. So we find a child always expecting persecution and perhaps becoming aggressive in self-defense against

imagined attack. This is an illness, but the pattern can be found as a phase in the development of almost any child" (Winnicott, 1984, p. 94).

It would seem that antisocial behaviour has deep underpinnings rooted not only in internal psychodynamic factors, but also in a missing aptitude to guide natural aggression in a way that allows it to become useful. When "bad" aspects of the self become disavowed and split off internally, reflecting an outer tendency to want to repress the unacceptable aspects of human behaviour, there is nowhere for these disturbances to be contained and unfolded. The more alienated these parts become, the more desperate they are for contact, eventually calling attention to themselves through extreme behaviours. Sadly, these acts do not even then bring the kind of attention that would be positively transformative, but instead draw further reprisals and misunderstanding, resulting in increased alienation for all concerned.

Intrapsychic dynamics

Although the experiences of shame, grandiosity, power, and revenge are inextricably linked, they will be introduced individually here in order to explore each of them in depth. The most pertinent aspects in relation to the field of school violence will be included, while bearing in mind that each dynamic is a rich area of exploration much broader than is relevant to our discussion here.

Shame

In 1895 Freud first wrote about shame as a defense and a cause of repression. He identified shame as an affect (fear) within a social context where others would know about a matter of self-reproach. In attempting to define shame he realized that shame was multifaceted and came up with a three-pronged view of shame as a social or interpersonal affect linked with being observed by another; a defense against the memory of a source of unpleasure; and as a symptom of self-reproach. Thus shame could be seen as affect, defense, or symptom (Morrison, 1989). Kohut uses the term "nameless shame" in respect to mortification, disturbed self-acceptance, and dejection. According to Kohut a definition of shame must account for disappointment, failure, and deficit (Morrison 1989).

Three types of shame are identified. Overt shame which is consciously experienced shame; unidentified or unacknowledged shame, where shame has been experienced by the individual but remains unconscious; and bypassed shame, where shame is circumvented into obsessiveness about the self (Ayers, 2000). Shame can be seen in social anxiety, sense of inferiority, narcissistic injury, embarrassment, or dread (Wurmser, 1997). As a sense of identity develops, emphasis is placed on the experience of selfhood and on measuring up to internalized ideals created by the self. In not measuring up to this ideal self, shame is the experience of failure of the self to attain the goals it sets as an ideal (Morrison, 1989). When one is viewed in a perceived derogatory way, the shamed is in relation to a shamer, generating a sense of unlovability or of low self-worth, and a fear of being despised. Failure may induce a sense of profound helplessness and unlovability and can lead to withdrawal.

"Shame is experienced as a blow to one's self-image, which leads to secrecy and concealment of one's being" (Ayers, 2000, p. 37). Concealing one's being, not only from others but also from oneself, leads to increasing isolation and alienation. Unable to make oneself visible as a result of the shame experienced, the individual hides behind apparently harsh behaviours when attempting to connect. This behaviour is frequently observed in the behaviour of both the school bully and those who are bullied or ostracized. Here is an example.

Melanie is a 13 year-old adolescent female who, being deemed unattractive and repulsive by her peers, has been generally rejected by the various cliques at her middle school. Despite being obnoxious and hateful to the other kids, she has attached herself to a classmate, June, who has at times been kind to her. Melanie follows June around during recess, imposing herself on the small group of friends who usually sit together for lunch, even though she is unwanted there. One of June's close friends, Jennifer, is an engaging, intelligent, and popular girl to whom Melanie has taken a strong dislike. Jennifer herself had been horribly teased and rejected during her earlier years at elementary school and is now ultra-sensitive to this kind of behaviour.

On a daily basis, Melanie singles Jennifer out in such places as the school bathroom, the library, or the playground, making taunting remarks to her. She publicly calls her names, saying that she is trash and a slut, throwing things at her, and belittling her in many ways. Jennifer, due to her past experience, finds herself unable to defend herself becoming re-traumatized at these attacks. Although the school counsellor has been brought in to help with the situation no change has occurred in the frequency of the daily attacks on Jennifer.

One day, after a particularly virulent attack, Jennifer uses new insight gained in a therapeutic session with me. She manages to engage with Melanie. She says, "Melanie I know that the only way you can make connection with me is to throw things at me and make horrible remarks to me. I know that underneath your attacks on me you really want to make contact with me. Well, here I am now—I'm right here. How does it feel? Now I challenge you to be real with me. Here is a chance to really connect. I know that you're probably really ashamed of being excluded by everyone. Tell me about it. How does it feel?" Going on in this vein, Jennifer after some minutes elicits tears from Melanie who begins to sob. In meeting Melanie in an authentic way and recognizing her deeper emotional experience, Jennifer is able to create a container in which Melanie can make contact with her deep sadness and allow it to be seen.

Jennifer, being a particularly mature and insightful adolescent had managed to engage successfully with Melanie, using her ability to contain her own emotions while drawing Melanie out. The opportunity that Jennifer had in personal therapy to process her own pain around being bullied, as well as having found a supportive container for her own anger and vengeful tendencies, had left her in a place where she was able to understand Melanie's actions and respond to her from a more neutral place in herself. Had she not done her own inner work with my support as her therapist, she may have remained withdrawn and frozen, inwardly terrified and hateful, as is generally the case with students who are either under attack or excluded from social groups. This case example illustrates well how containment and understanding for disavowed emotions allows them to transform when finding support.

With some individuals fleeting feelings of shame may conceal a fundamental feeling that one is in some way defective and unlovable down to the core of one's being. "An individual then becomes petrified by the movements of life; a way of being that is plagued by the polarized feelings of non-existence and the fear of having one's existence destroyed by a glance" (Ayers, 2000, p. 11). The fear of becoming exposed or visible when one is not ready for this rests on the feeling of being observed in a way that finds one lacking. The observer may be an objective perceiver or an internalized aspect of the self. Erosive doubt accumulates due to the voices of doubt and humiliation that shatter and distort the self and that haunt one with derision and doubt on an ongoing basis (Bion, 1957). The narcissistically vulnerable part, which is so sensitive to humiliation and exclusion, clamours for complete need fulfilment. The shattered parts despite being projected outward, continue to visit and haunt one. In order to release the tension of the unbearable experience of exclusion, and in order to avoid the violence associated with this trauma, the "other" is demeaned or demonized, allowing one to find a place of power and relative safety. The shattered self attempts to avoid the scathing gaze of others by doing them, or oneself, harm through rage and violence (Anderson, 2007). The ability to discern the exclusionary act or derogation is lacking, and there is therefore no protection against the voices of doubt and humiliation. Projection of the demeaned part on to others only provides temporary relief.

Shame and identity only become linked when one is able to articulate a shame experience. Shame arises at a critical moment when the interpersonal bridge with a significant other is ruptured, thus cutting off a source of enjoyment and understanding. This loss of the interpersonal bridge is the original source of pain. The individual, cut off, begins to sense increasing alienation and rage entrenching the separation and preventing reconnection. The self is then viewed as defective and is disowned. As a result the other becomes both desired and hated. The shame cannot be articulated. A distorted sense of identity ensues with the denial of needs and feelings often leading to splitting (Kaufman, 1992). The internal perpetuation of shame occurs through the splitting process where part of oneself attacks other negative aspects of self. Not only does the hatred get expressed toward those who incur the pain, but also toward the self, which is deemed unworthy.

It can be seen that shame results from both an internal and external source. The one who is hated or demeaned may be attacked internally as a process of internalization of the shamer occurs, resulting in self-hatred. Shame may also be projected outward on to another as blame and hostility. The "other" then becomes the one or many who are hated and derogated. Shame may result in withdrawal and isolation sometimes leading to suicide, or in outward attacks and violent reprisals as occur in bullying and school shootings.

In listening to Kip Kinkel's confession (PBS, 1998) one notices how these dynamics occurred for him. A number of times during the police interview Kinkel sobbed that he wished that he had killed himself instead of the others. When being arrested he had threatened the arresting officer with a knife that had been strapped to his leg in the hope that, "I would have been shot dead". Throughout the interview, Kip expressed his desire to be dead. His self-hatred becomes evident in his repeated expressions of wanting himself dead. When asked why he had killed his father, Kip replied that he could not face his father's continued shaming of him when Kip was expelled from school.

"My dad kept saying how my mom—(sobbing loudly)—how embarrassed she was going to be, and how horrible I was—(more sobbing)—and I couldn't let my mom feel like that. I couldn't do anything else. There was no other way. I had no other choice. It was the only thing I could do" (PBS, 1998).

Rather than allowing the shaming to continue Kip had killed both of his parents. He had also killed and wounded others at his school. He could give no explanation for his actions other than that there was something wrong with his head. He identified as loving his parents, but knew that he could not allow them to be shamed by his expulsion from school. Kip's own shame, in becoming intolerable, is projected on to his parents, particularly his mother, and in order to get rid of the pain of exposure, he kills those he perceives as suffering from it, attempting to rid himself of it at the same time. In this dreadful way, Kip Kinkel, attempted to empower himself in an intolerable situation, exacting in his mind, a strange sort of justice and retribution. Rather than there being an opportunity for Kip to share his pain with another in an humanitarian way, rather than there being a context in which Kip could have felt contained through some sort of conveyed understanding or attempt at treatment, Kip was sentenced to 111 years in adult prison, without the possibility of parole.

Grandiosity, power, and revenge

Incidences of narcissistic rage are attempts to get rid of experiences of shame. The experience of shame becomes almost intolerable and as a defense, a world of violent fantasies develops. These fantasies contain figures and themes of grandiosity and power. The withdrawal into fantasy allows the individual to replace his failed social world with this fantasy world. Compensatory fantasy provides an effective coping mechanism in restoring a sense of self. The fantasies realize illusions of omnipotent control and can lead to gratification of desires for revenge (Meloy, 1988). Feelings of shame are relieved by the need for revenge against those associated with the injury, at which time the grandiose sense of self is restored. Revenge and associated empowerment bring some identity and meaning into an individual's life, providing a sense of importance in a situation where that person most likely feels humiliated or worthless (Frankl, 1984). As an example we might look at Virginia Tech mass killer Seung-Hui Cho, reaching out from his grave through an 1,800-word manifesto, 28 video and audio clips, and 43 still pictures in his attempt to become recognized as a person of power and import. In this multimedia package he warned, "I will no longer run". "When the time came, I did it. I had to". An angry Cho railed about the debaucheries of the rich and described the two Columbine High School killers as martyrs. He compared himself to Jesus and while brandishing weapons flaunted himself in a variety of powerful postures. His obviously grandiose posturing and verbal messages appear to increasingly inflate him as he continues his message to the world. In portraying himself through these media, he succeeds in justifying his importance to both himself and his listeners.

Grandiosity

Alfred Adler writes of a human propensity toward anti-social behaviour. Behind every inferiority complex lies a hidden superiority complex, which he equates as a claim to perfection. The conscious willing self is not aware of the superiority complex. The inner enemy is that superiority claim that you don't even know that you've got, but that is destroying you and those around you. The individual acts out of a private logic with which he expects the entire world to cooperate. The goal is to be higher than other people and in depreciating others there may be an acting out in anti-social ways, seeking to gain superiority, but unknowingly. The human quest for significance becomes dominant. The cause of human destructiveness rests on superiority claims found in the superiority complex of the individual (Adler, 1929).

> "Organization of the self becomes grandiose as a result of fragmentation, resulting in crazy grandiose claims being made for oneself. Becoming possessed by grandiosity gets a person when they feel alone. It is almost as if a powerful spell is able to make the ego believe that it is the grandiose "I" without any awareness of being possessed. It makes a perfect replica of the person that is really not one, while one has no sense of being under any spell. Enchantment and the power of the spell is key here. This seductive power is referred to as the Demon Lover" (Moore, 1989, tape 4).

The demon lover aspect often appears in an eroticized and seductive form that pulls one in due to its claim to the godhead, the numinous power. This demonic aspect holds a bogus god claim, and promises to the individual something that it cannot deliver. It promises order and delivers chaos, promises life but delivers death. The bogus god claim is always destructive as the individual would rather have the entire cosmos disappear than not be god. This description matches so well the attitude and behaviour of Seung-Hui Cho as described above.

In school situations where students have been singled out for exclusion, bullying, or teacher discrimination, strong feelings of isolation and loneliness result from the rejection. When this occurs repeatedly, a strong need develops to reassert oneself and remedy the situation. This need is also fanned by desperation to avoid the pain of the situation. The hatred that grows at the ongoing persecution and rejection by peers seeks revenge, and the grandiose self only feels restored when violent retaliation of some sort occurs. If the individual does not develop a strong ego-self axis when the self is diminished with a grandiose defense, self-inflation and compulsion, with an inability to experience any self-satisfaction occur. This sounds like Satan who is never satisfied, is always empty and in pain, and is always full of hate and envy. It is always related to power in the shadow (Moore, 1989, tape 3). All of this is unconscious for the individual who will not have a sense that, "I am not doing this; I do not know why I am doing that; I don't reflect on what I am doing or why I am doing it; I just act out in an aggressive or sexual way. I am just into doing it." Compulsive behaviours like these reflect the ego's experience of id dominance, an inner instinctive entity, which clearly does what it wants to do. These entities tend to be infinitely grandiose, reflected in the lack of adherence to rules and the impulsivity of wanting everything now. Looking at compulsions through this lens, one can see this radical grandiose desire wanting to gobble up reality. In this way the hole left by wounding is filled.

> "The grandiose may also be a defense against damaged self-concept. This is achieved by stripping off and externalizing all bad traits. The person develops blind hatred towards many others who are assigned subhuman status. Such a person does not recognize that others also have a right to exist. There is a destructive readiness to injure others on the grounds that they are monsters who have no right to survive. Viewing others as monsters is a dissociative defense, in which the human qualities of a person are forgotten. The self is elevated over the monster who is bad and so can safely feel contempt as well as disgust and rage towards these traits" (Dwivedi, 1993, p. 67).

A sense of security in one's own subjective conviction of one's perfection is established and one feels one's superiority over others, not through being related to them, but through holding on to this perfectionist self-image out of fear of truly seeing oneself as lacking, as reflected in the eyes of others (Fromm, 1973). An extreme form of this is illustrated in the dream of a patient as follows.

> "I have made a great invention, the "superdestroyer". It is a machine which, if one secret button is pushed that I alone know, can destroy all life in North America within the first hour, and within the next hour all life on earth. I alone, knowing the formula of the chemical substance, can protect myself. (Next scene). I have pushed the button; I notice no more life, I am alone, I feel exuberant" (Fromm, 1973, p. 372).

Grandiosity brings the individual an illusory experience of power, particularly in situations where the sense of self is diminished or where there is a pervasive inferiority complex established over time. Revenge too is a way of gaining power for the individual when a deep underlying hurt is covered over by rage and a desire to get back at the other and achieve reparation.

Power and revenge

Rage, violence, rebellion, oppression, and many other similar dynamics, are closely connected to both power and revenge. For those who are stripped of power, violent or vengeful acts are often the means used to restore strength and find a position of power within a disempowering situation. Like Adler, Hannah Arendt (1970) suggests that the cause of human destructiveness rests on superiority claims found in the superiority complex of the individual. This reflects the tendency for impotence to breed violence and for loss of power to become a temptation to substitute violence for power. In the expression of violence, power is once again gained, although this is likely to be temporary. Some violence is driven primarily by "the will to power" (Diamond, 1996, p. 9). Chronic feelings of victimization, insignificance, alienation, and thwarted entitlement often lead to attempts to restore acknowledgement and inclusion through an act so desperate or violent, that it will draw attention to the instigator of the act. In achieving this, one is again able to feel empowered and gain position within the context in which one has been previously ignored or rendered powerless.

> Julie is in the fourth grade at school. She has mostly been ignored or made fun of by the other children due to her physical appearance, which is unkempt and obese. Julie was taken in by her grandmother when her mother's drug problem became too severe for her to care for Julie any longer. She hates her grandmother who is emotionally cruel to her, but at the same time fears losing her as grandmother is the only source of security that Julie has. Julie feels disempowered in her relationship with her grandmother as her ideas or preferences are not given any credence. Life is lived strictly according to grandmother's rules with no allowance for Julie's feelings or points of view. Similarly at school, Julie feels disregarded in her peer group. She has no

relationships with her peers and spends her free time at school alone. Despite the fact that she has tried to make friends summoning up her courage to approach some of the girls in her year, the other kids continue to ignore or deprecate her.

One day at school one of the kids in Julie's class accidentally bumped her, causing Julie to drop the books and writing materials she was carrying. Without apologizing, the other child hurried by leaving Julie to pick up all her belongings on her own. For Julie this was the last straw. She began to yell and scream uncontrollably, throwing objects around the room, pounding her fists on the desks and kicking out at objects on the floor. Screaming, she ran out of the door heading for the street, knocking other children over in her mad dash toward the busy street outside.

With the teacher and some of the children chasing after her, and gathering more attention as she ran, Julie had found a moment of power. With all eyes on her, she had become the centre of attention. By the time Julie was apprehended and taken to the principal's office, she had received more attention than she had ever had in her life. She was elated.

Stephen Diamond (1996) describes this kind of situation well. "We are all apt on occasion to feel outraged at the apparently arbitrary facts of our essentially insecure, often painful, and sometimes, seemingly meaningless, insignificant existence. We rebel–at least inwardly if not outwardly—against our human destiny" (p. 26). In rebelling, a desperate act or expression restores a sense of power and significance. In feeling victimized by circumstances, others, society, and culture, perpetrators of violence such as mass killers and school shooters, are unable to assert their power in the world. In committing violent acts they assume their power and momentarily become powerful victimizers rather than powerless victims.

Revenge surfaces when marginalized groups or individuals can no longer tolerate remaining unheard and unrecognized by mainstream positions (Mindell, 1995). Revenge is often the only means of getting attention for what they suffer at the hands of those who are unconscious of what they are going through. In order to be heard and noticed behaviour escalates until eventually the pain and fury experienced by the marginalized may emerge through acts of extreme violence such as acts of terrorism and mass killings. Taking revenge and committing acts of vengeful destructiveness are spontaneous reactions to intense and unjustified suffering inflicted by another. The desire for vengeance may build up over a period of time with revenge fantasies occurring frequently, although not acted upon until finally the act of revenge takes place. "Revenge is of much greater intensity than a defensive aggression, and is often cruel, lustful, and insatiable" (Fromm, 1973, p. 304). In getting back at the one who has committed the painful or atrocious act, taking vengeance not only restores power to the avenger, but also allows for an experience of reparation. The fundamental sense of injustice harboured as a result of being treated badly can be perceived as evened out when revenge is taken.

> "Man seems to take justice into his own hands, when God or secular authorities fail. It is as if in the passion for vengeance he elevates himself to the role of God, and of the angels of vengeance. The act of vengeance may be his greatest hour just because of this self-elevation" (*ibid* p. 306).

Through the act of revenge, the unheard become heard, justice is restored, the abhorrent crime is magically undone, and the powerless gain power in a situation where they have been previously unrecognized. Revenge then becomes an act of reparation, restoring value in the self through avenging the hurt done to it.

When the self is perceived as diminished or failing to measure up to an expected ideal, the resultant relationship with oneself and others becomes impaired. The shame that occurs engenders various reactions. Self-hatred and disparagement may result in alienation and withdrawal or alternately, in expressed aggression toward others. This may take the form of violent fantasies that are eventually acted out, or acts of revenge aimed at hurting and diminishing the other in order to feel exalted oneself. In attempting to be better or higher than others in order to avoid the pain of diminishment, a grandiose view of oneself may develop in order to escape from feelings of inferiority. A false sense of being perfect allows experiences of self-worth and brings an experience of power. Through violent acts of revenge, or retribution momentarily bringing self-value and reparation for the wrongs done, shame disappears temporarily. However it does resurface when the wounding is again touched upon, or when violent acts result in further humiliation and shame. All of these dynamics are evident in the experiences and expressions of alienated youth in the school system. If this cycle is caught early enough reparation may be gained through the offer of support and empathy inculcating a sense of being valued and allowing a milieu in which to share feelings and gain an understanding of what is truly happening on an inner level. Acts of violence may never need to happen then as pent-up emotions are released and responsibility shared by others in the system.

Hatred, rage, and envy

The likelihood of aggression and envy in the young child adds to a predisposition to violence. Feelings of being unloveable, insignificant, and inferior, in addition to experiences of helplessness, mobilize rage and hatred (Akhtar, Kramer & Parens, 1995). The aggression that some parents hold in abeyance while their children are still helpless, dependent, and controllable, manifests once the children reach adolescence with a concomitant experience on the part of the child associated with unworthiness and unloveability. In addition, the resentment and hostility that many parents feel for the young infant for stealing their lives away, are internalized by the infant, resulting not only in a developing self-hatred, but also destructive tendencies toward the hating and hateful object. This pattern is repeated later in life when once again confronted by someone else who has a rejecting or aggressive attitude.

Hatred and rage

Freud (Akhtar et al. 1995) viewed hatred as a response emanating from the ego when it abhors and attempts to destroy all that is a source of displeasure for it. All unpleasant experiences such as need, fear, or frustration, give rise to destructive aggression. If hatred is viewed as existing on a continuum of experience, milder forms may emerge as a desire to make the hated object suffer, or the need to control, coerce, or subjugate the source of unpleasantness, whereas the more extreme experiences of hatred may result in overt destructive acts. In some situations hatred is considered an acceptable reaction, such as in situations of war where there is an identified enemy whom one is allowed to hate. In other situations where hatred is not sanctioned by the social context, such as in hatred of one's fellow school students or teachers, hatred has to be strongly defended against, and as a result may become split off from the conscious mind of the individual. Here the feelings of hatred remain hidden, disguised, or projected elsewhere. Continued splitting off of these emotions can result in complete fragmentation of the self.

Hatred can be object-directed, self-directed, or internalized through identification with hated or hating objects (Kernberg, 1992). Hatred is viewed as a universal response, mobilized and directed when threat or potential injury is perceived toward oneself or one's love objects. A delicate balance exists between love and hate, as well as between the capacity for defense, control, and regulation, and the intensity of rage or hate experienced. Hate may be activated and connected to rage to the degree associated with internal conflict, traumatic injury, or narcissistic wounding. Although hate may be present without rage, the two often go together. "Hatred is a complex, structured derivative of the affect rage that expresses several wishes: to destroy a bad object, to make it suffer, and to control it" (Kernberg, 1995). Functions of rage are to eliminate sources of irritation or pain, or to eliminate an obstacle to gratification.

> "Hatred thus emerges as the more primitive, more direct derivative of rage in response to the experience of suffering pain or aggression: envy emerges as a special form of hatred under conditions of a relationship in which highly desirable and teasingly withheld aspects of the object complicate the experience of rageful frustration" (p. 67).

A consequence of hatred is its justification as revenge toward the object, manifesting in the desire to hurt, destroy, or dominate the perceived instigator. The wish for revenge and sadism go hand in hand.

> "Factors that inhibit aggression and restrain violence against the self and others are likely to undergo more alteration in traumatized individuals. Greater psychological distance, psychological alienation and dehumanization of the "enemy" facilitates socially sanctioned mayhem and murder" (Blum, 1995, p. 27).

When the victimized individual is unable to find support to safely express the hatred and aggression felt toward the victimizer as a result of the trauma experienced, this violence is likely to burst out in an unsanctioned manner, often in a surprising and devastating way. Not only is the victim persecuted by the aggression directed toward him, he may at some point become the victimizer by retaliating toward those who have done him harm. This was shown in the case of Stella who threatened her victimizers with her penknife, and in the many instances of school shootings that have occurred. Anxiety and the developed sense of helplessness are relieved through this role reversal.

When there is an expectation or belief that conditions could be changed, and are not, rage arises. It is here that one's sense of justice is offended, and resorting to the violence that arises from the experienced rage becomes enormously tempting due to the swift and immediate retaliatory/retributive factor within the violent outburst (Arendt, 1970). In this way the intensity of rage and hatred may result in denial of hatred by the cutting off of all feeling including hatred, or by transforming aggression into retaliatory action.

Aggressive acts can be seen as a way of desperately attempting to make contact with others, especially when rejected and alienated. The experienced hatred needs to be received, to be tolerated, and to be survived both by oneself and by others. It is when hatred can be perceived objectively, that objective love can be reached. When an individual is deeply disturbed, love can only be reached through permitting the hate (Winnicott, 1976). When love is present and the capacity for it is sufficiently developed it allows both successful splitting between the loved and the hated, and also successful eventual integration of the two. On the social level the evolution of culture is ultimately determined by the amount of love, understanding, and freedom experienced by its children.

> "Only love produces the self-integration and individuation needed for cultural innovation. Every abandonment, every betrayal, every hateful act toward children returns tenfold a few decades later upon the historical stage, while every empathic act that helps a child become what he or she wants to become, heals society and moves it in unexpected wondrous new directions" (deMause, 2002, p. 59).

Those who show self-destructive or antisocial tendencies almost always evidence strong envy within the context of intense hatred. The object of hatred and envy is often perceived as possessing qualities that are judged as desirable or good, the very qualities that are perceived as missing in, and sought after by the hating individual. The amount of envy intensifies according to the degree that the individual feels excluded and overlooked. Rage and hatred are heaped upon those who are envied.

Envy

The word envy comes from the Latin *invideo*, which means to look maliciously or spitefully into, to begrudge, to cast an evil eye upon. Envy is a major manifestation of human aggression. The origin of envy lies in the need to spoil and destroy the object that is also needed for survival, and is actually the object of love. Envy is the angry feeling that another person possesses and enjoys something desirable that one does not have—the envious impulse being to take it away or to spoil it (Klein, 1988, p. 181).

Envy arises when exposed to others who possess that which one desires but does not have. This is particularly so with individuals who are experiencing deprivation. Envy is constellated in the child and adolescent when exposed to desired objects that are either unavailable or rejecting. Examples of peer rejection, teacher discrimination, and bullying are all factors that may spark envy of those who appear to belong and fit in with others. Envy is directed toward those who deny the desired relationship or support, and also to the qualities of friendship and solidarity perceived as being inhabited by them. The effects of envy and the development of greed related to the envy experienced influence both internal and external perceptions of the other in a corrosive manner. Envy is therefore closely linked to hatred and desire for retribution.

Another factor contributing to envy is the desire to be freed from destructive impulses and persecutory anxiety. Children and adolescents in the school environment who are experiencing difficult emotions may perceive others as being free from anxiety and the torment of negative impulses. The individual desires this liberation, but not finding it in herself, envies and hates those perceived as possessing it. A child who has a deep-rooted relationship with a positive model can withstand temporary states of envy and hatred due to the capacity for love and gratitude learned through the supportive relationship. "It is *enjoyment*, and the *gratitude* to which it gives rise, that mitigate destructive impulses, envy and greed. It is when there is an inability to build up a good and secure internal object that security and a stable foundation on which to build a strong ego are lacking" (Klein, 1988, p. 187). Then states such as hatred and envy have a rich and fertile soil in which to grow and abound. Children who are most susceptible to the effects of bullying and exclusion by others may therefore be the ones who have been unable to develop an internal stability and ego strength due to the lack of internalization of a positive object. This may not only be the result of object relationships from the past, but may also occur in the present where a need for support is not met either internally or externally within the school context. One would like to think that the presence of another person who could become a good object for the disturbed child, could help to alleviate some of the repercussions of the wounding and provide a model for internalization and enhancement of ego strength. This might be a teacher who is understanding and acknowledging of the child's difficulties and approaches the student in a loving and supportive way. This could also take the form of an older student filling the role of mentor for the child. These roles are mostly lacking within the school environment.

In looking at pathology in relational terms, the process that occurs is described as follows.

> "Those processes by which a child takes on the badness that appears to be in the hurtful objects of his environment are compensatory. Rather than having bad objects in his environment, the child controls the badness by becoming bad himself through internalization of these bad objects. This process of splitting and internalizing tends to make the environment good, but now the child has the internalized bad objects within himself. The child further defends against these inner bad objects or persecutors by repression, which banishes the bad objects to the unconscious. If these internalized bad objects are sufficiently charged, and if repression fails, they may cause psychological problems in various ways." (St. Clair 2000, p. 59).

Splitting of good and bad parts can be seen to be one of the fundamental defences against persecutory anxiety. Confusion develops between the self and the other who comes to stand for the self. Bound up with this is a weakening of the ego and a grave disturbance in relationships. This dynamic can be observed in Kip Kinkel's confusion in which he is unable to differentiate between experiences of his parents and his own.

In experiences constellating ongoing envy in the individual, the capacity for gratitude and happiness is thwarted. The insatiable desire to have for oneself denied experiences or relationships, leads to intense internal conflict and often self-hatred. Attempts are made to repress the envious and hostile parts within oneself. In some cases the individual may be successful at doing this, only to have these parts erupt in destructive attacks at some later point. In others, the expression of destructive criticism brings sadistic pleasure while also exacerbating internal experiences of self-hatred. Love and a need for connection may become irrevocably intertwined with hatred and envy leading to confusion and disturbed relationships. Envy is inextricably tied up with the unrequited longing for love and the urgent need to be protected from the consequences of one's own destructive impulses. Without these inherent needs being met, a fertile ground for the breeding of destructive fantasies develops often resulting in the acting out of aggressive and violent behaviour.

Summary

In this chapter relevant psychodynamic factors contributing to experiences of alienation and violence among school youth have been explored. The purpose of this chapter has been to illuminate these factors in the hope that greater understanding of underlying dynamics may aid in containment of disturbing and potentially violent emotions and behaviours encountered within the school environment. Containment would provide the means to support children who have been ostracized and excluded, and who suffer from internalized self-hatred and conflict. Enhanced understanding of the internalized experiences of these children would hopefully also reduce punitive patterns found not only in the school system, but also in socio-cultural attitudes toward alienated or violent youth. Not only would this enhanced understanding contribute to preventive interventions in working with youth, but if applied in practical ways, would also be effective in dealing with the aftermath of behaviours such as those found in bullying and other school violence.

The following dynamics have been attended to in this chapter.

- Children who have been deprived of good enough provision in their lives are more prone to maladjustment. An unconscious attempt to have the world acknowledge and repair the injury may result in antisocial behaviour. The hope behind the disturbance is that the true self will have a chance to emerge and be recognized.
- Disconnection with the self occurs when the self is not sufficiently adaptive to deal with change or stress. The alienated self can only communicate through disturbance and attempts to gain attention through acts of aggression and hatred.
- The pain that the individual experiences when deprived or disconnected, often results in self-blame, shame, and self-hatred, leading to psychic retreat and further alienation.
- Shame may be both intrapsychic or interpersonal. In both cases it is connected with failure to achieve ideals. The inability to achieve perfection is associated with self-castigation and the tendency to diminish the self, with a resultant concealment of one's being. This furthers the experience of isolation.
- The alienated and shattered self attempts to avoid pain and humiliation through the expression of rage and violence. Projection on others provides protection against the shattering humiliation and shame experienced.
- When shame is experienced internally or in interpersonal interaction, the deficiency experienced is projected on to others, establishing a grandiose self to offset the deep internal inadequacy experienced. Grandiosity restores power to the self, although this is not a reflection of true power.
- Acts of revenge restore a sense of power to the individual who experiences victimization, providing reparation to the wounded and hidden parts of the self. Due to underlying anger, hatred, and envy, revenge may take violent forms.
- Rage, hatred, and envy are commonly associated with experiences of alienation when one's sense of justice is affronted.

Violent outbursts provide a retributive factor, relieving the self of unconscious destructive impulses connected to shame, humiliation, and the longing for unrequited love and acceptance.

• Acts of bullying and violence create a way in which to make contact with others where no other means are accessible. This serves to temporarily break the spell of alienation.

A deepened understanding of the psychodynamic factors effecting troubled youth allows us to notice when individual children are alienated and suffering. Enhanced insight into these factors increases the possibility of engaging more effectively with them in times of trouble, both before the eruption of violence and after violent acts are perpetrated. Providing a container in which disavowed material can be expressed and acknowledged, relieves both the individual from carrying this burden alone and alerts others to systemic symptomatology.

The purpose of this chapter has been to provide greater insight into the underlying intrapsychic dynamics that disturb children and adolescents within the context of the school system. It is hoped that this will lead to more effective ways of both preventing and dealing with problems that arise in order to alleviate much of the suffering that occurs for individuals, families, and members of the system when encountering the painful effects of alienation and violence. The lens that this exploration provides will hopefully deepen awareness of the dynamics involved, provide containment for disavowed experiences in order to break through the defenses present, and lead to the development of facilitative interventions for all concerned.

CHAPTER SIX

Group dialogue and the quantum field

One of the most potent ways of defusing challenging and disturbing situations is through group dialogue. The opportunity to talk about difficult issues and problems is invaluable as both a preventive and interventive measure in times of potential or escalating violence. Children, who are having problems in the school setting, benefit enormously from being able to find support and understanding for their experiences. This of course can occur on a one-to-one level, but it is in the group situation that the individual child or adolescent can find her own experience mirrored in the sharing of others, thus breaking through often-experienced self-judgment, alienation, and isolation. Hearing group members talk of similar inner experiences to oneself, relieves the individual of the burden of carrying something deemed monstrous that appears to belong only to oneself. The group dialogue format also provides a milieu in which all levels of a system can interact creating a bridge between the various populations contained within the larger structure that usually have no contact with each other. This is valuable in expanding the identity of the system and in cultivating an attitude that includes and acknowledges the views of all its members.

Any enduring society must be grounded upon recognition of the motivating desires of the individual and of the group (Follett, 1965). A democratic way of life involves working towards an honest integration of all points of view. Social phenomena are a continuous process, which are always changing, and every human activity and decision is "not a thing in itself, but merely a moment in a process" (p. 15). Parker Follett equates conflict with continued, unintegrated difference and sees conflict as constructive and neither good nor bad. She uses the term "integration" to describe her method of exploring and resolving difference as compared to compromise. "Compromise does not create, it deals with what already exists; integration creates something new which can be applied to the disturbance to make it constructive. Integration is a method of bringing differences out into the open" (p. 35). In order to be a democrat we need to learn how to live with other humans. Progress itself depends on the group, and the group is the basis of a progressive and workable social psychology. Problems can be solved by the subtle process of the intermingling of all the different ideas of the group. What evolves from the group process is a composite idea, rather than my idea or your idea, and "I" then represents the whole, rather than one part of it. Something new is created. The essence of the group process is an acting and reacting; a process which brings out differences and integrates them into a unity. The complex reciprocal action, the interweaving of the members of the group, is the social process. The core of the social process is the harmonizing of difference through interpenetration.

Deep democracy

The approach that I use in working with groups is based on the principle of deep democracy, "that special feeling or belief in the inherent importance of all parts of ourselves and all viewpoints in the world around us" (Mindell, 1992). Deep democracy supports even those parts, expressions, or experiences that are usually pushed away, disowned, or marginalized by individuals and societies. When all the parts can be honoured and viewed as valuable and necessary, a forum can be created in which previously unheard voices find a place for expression. Not only is deep democracy a valuable approach in dealing with the outer world, it is also an integral part of inner development, and challenges us to open up to everything in our inner and outer universes (*ibid* p. 9). In providing an environment in which diverse experiences, even those frowned upon, can be supported and heard, individuals reveal what has been previously hidden or unknown. This leads to the expression, acknowledgement, and sharing of emotions usually held secret, deepening the connection between those present.

The idea of deep democracy can be seen to parallel Plato's utopian view of community (Hamilton & Cairns, 1961). This community is an organic entity in which citizens are like the cells in a body where all parts are equally important. All parts of a system need to be valued. Without the presence of all the different parts and positions, interactions and growth will remain incomplete. Overlooked and excluded parts will emerge in a way that disrupt overall functioning of the system. If they are not heard and included they can escalate rapidly and result in attacks and outbursts. Disturbance arises from the whole system and cannot be blamed on one part, person, or event, but on the lack of integration within the system as a whole. This way of thinking can be very aptly applied to the school system. Through incidents of school shootings we can readily see how the emotional reactions of individuals who have been excluded rapidly escalate to be expressed in terrorist acts. Although these individuals are identified as the "problem" we have seen in previous chapters how the whole system may also contribute to the disruption.

People hold a more or less unconscious drive to develop the less known aspects of themselves in the push to realize and live their entire potential. Interactions among us provide a ground in which this can happen. The incentive behind disturbance and conflict provides us with an opportunity to become more of who we truly are, awakening our awareness to newly emerging information, and expanding individual and group identity. The impulse to be powerful, win, love, and connect often provokes confrontation (Mindell, 1992). Because we usually only identify with one form of behaviour or belief system and try to negate the existence of others outside of this, conflicts between parts arise and escalate. In the processing of these situations we are provided with opportunities to learn more about ourselves, others, and the social system in which we live. In this way inclusiveness and understanding of previously disavowed aspects can be cultivated and developed, illustrating the principles of deep democracy. This process may also contribute to a sense of connection between previously opposed individuals and groups.

The field

A field is defined as the atmosphere or climate of any community or system, including its physical, environmental, and emotional surroundings. The field can be envisioned as a huge anthropos figure, every cell of which can give rise to all of creation. Similar to the holographic paradigm of David Bohm (1980), every part is seen to reflect and also contain the whole. As everyday reality unfolds from an interconnected wholeness, each particle emerging from wholeness reflects and interconnects with every other particle. The Bell experiment shows quantum entanglement or interconnectedness, sometimes called the "unity of the world", as manifesting in two or more quantum entities, originally part of the same system, even when subsequently separated in time and space (Mindell, 2000). Each field is in a constant process of transformation and evolution, initially manifesting through chaos and polarization. The atmosphere or field in which we live is seen to be electromagnetic, and as such it arranges the contents of the field around poles, just as a magnet organizes iron filings around the magnetic poles (Mindell, 2000). Polarization in turn gives each position a chance to "wrestle" with the other, thus promoting an alchemical shift that often appears as a change in feeling, position, and value system. Out of this is born a deeper understanding and empathy for those holding initially opposing views and positions, as well as for estranged parts of the self. Within a group setting one may find that various roles emerge, are held by different group members, interact with each other, and then transform. Noticing these roles and being aware of what they imply for the whole system, adds awareness to how individuals may be reflecting aspects of the overall contentious issue. The different roles are meaningful and important for the whole group. As group members interact with each other more is learned about the inherent experiences of each role or position and what it may be trying to express. This awakens us to experiences previously held secret due to perceived judgments against them. A good example of this is provided in chapter three. Despite a role in the field that strongly opposes violence of any kind, Gwen picks up an opposing position in sharing her murderous impulses towards people in general. In voicing her inner struggle with these polarities within herself, she opens the way for other members in the group to give expression to their own hatred of humanity. In negotiating between two points of view, one against violence and the other admitting to violent tendencies, a shared empathy among group members is cultivated. In Gwen opening up the role of the murderous one, the rest of the field becomes free to respond and interact, deepening the process of awareness on the issue.

Expression of the roles, and "wrestling" of polarities, supports the interaction of diverse points of view and gives rise to the emergence of underlying, unidentified material. It is through this interaction that transformation begins to occur. The group facilitator intentionally supports emerging roles in order to help their meaning emerge for the awareness of other group members, thus expanding the group's way of identifying itself. Here is an example.

Roy is an ungainly youth who describes himself as more interested in science fiction and computer technology than in relating to other humans. He is awkward in his communication attempts with the other kids and often keeps himself on the margins of the group. He shares that he has no friends and doesn't want any.

One day in group we begin a discussion about how some of the participants seem to do all the talking while others sit back and watch. One of the kids, Mark, who generally talks a lot, is the most vocal about this. He feels it is unfair that some people in the group sit idly and don't participate, placing more of a burden on those who do. He confronts Roy about his lack of engagement. Mark becomes angry when Roy does not respond to him continuing to sit quietly away from the group. Mark's voice begins to get louder and he begins to approach Roy in a menacing way. Roy shrinks back.

I make a facilitative intervention. I acknowledge Mark's experience, inviting him to say more about his feelings and views, supporting him to go further with his position. A couple of other kids join him in voicing their disquiet with the silent ones in group. I then ask for permission to support Roy's response. I stand beside Roy and invite him to respond. Although making an effort, he remains speechless and appears to be in a frozen state. I invite other group members to join Roy and speak about their own quietness. John begins to talk of his shyness and feelings of awkwardness in not fitting in. He shares how difficult it is for him to speak in front of other people and how he is afraid that other kids will make fun of him. I also share how difficult it was for me as a kid to talk in front of more than two people at a time and how I used to sit in silent pain when in a group. I look at Roy, making space for him to join us. He begins to talk about how his mother ridicules him for the way he looks and speaks, how useless he feels, and how cruel other kids are to him. He chooses to keep away from everyone, but is so lonely and unhappy. He really would like to reach out but is afraid.

As Roy speaks, the feeling in the room changes. A quiet descends, and I notice that some of the girls have tears in their eyes. Mark comes closer to Roy and holds out his hand. "Hey buddy," he says. "You can come hang out with me. You're okay—sorry I messed with you." He sits down next to Roy. The group discussion moves on, focused on experiences of loneliness and personal reactions to feeling alone.

In the above example, it can be seen how initially supporting Mark's position helped to de-escalate a potentially explosive situation. Supporting the roles held by Mark and Roy created an opportunity for the opposing positions to express more fully. Roy's role of the quiet or shy one was initially occupied by John, and then taken up by me. In filling the role of the shy one, an opening was made in which Mark's intolerance toward Roy's lack of engagement could be transformed into understanding and empathy. Similarly, hearing that others preferred him to speak out, Roy was given an opportunity to break through his isolation. The experience also transformed the whole group, deepening the way in which individuals perceived quietness and changing their relationship to it.

In addition to supporting roles that are present in the group, the facilitator may also draw attention to roles that are not represented or voiced. These are roles which might be present in the field, but which are not consciously recognized or directly expressed. These missing roles are often very important in processing contentious issues. For example, the role of the bully will often be unrepresented as fear of reprisal, rejection, or judgment may prevent one from speaking about personal experiences of being a bully. It is the facilitator's task then to attempt to encourage this role to speak out so that its experience can also be heard and supported, taking care to help others with their strong reactions to this position so as to avoid escalation and later scapegoating of the child who may be identified in that role. Once the individual holding the role begins to express her experience, the facilitator can help to deepen the awareness of what is held within this position through encouraging the sharing of feelings, opinions, and personal history. When these deep, often painful feelings are expressed, other group participants may be constellated to react to them, either by taking an oppositional or conflicting stance, or by beginning to understand more about the struggle of this individual. If conflict arises, a deeply democratic view will be used to encourage further dialogue between opposing positions until there is a deeper understanding of each side, creating transformation and the emergence of new awareness. The illumination of underlying layers of experience on each side leads to deep feeling shared by group members, supporting the ability to reach out to the previously denigrated individual. This can be seen in the example of Roy's experience described above.

Levels within the field

A group contains many levels of experience which contribute to its functioning. These levels are conceptualized as individual, relationship, subgroup, group, and systemic levels. When a group engages, a process can emerge on any or all of these levels, and any change that occurs will manifest through expression on one or more of these. Over the long-term, it can be seen that it would be useful for transformation to occur on all levels in order to achieve sustainable change. If one individual undergoes change and then comes back into a system that remains unchanged, regression may occur. Transformation can occur within a system through individual exploration as described in examples in chapters four and five, through relationship interaction as in the example of Roy and Mark above, or by processing roles and positions connected to a group's identity. It is within the large group that dynamics not usually found in any other group situation are constellated. The large group provides a wonderful opportunity to learn about the rich diversity present and how others, different to oneself, view and experience their world (de Mare, Piper & Thompson, 1991). It is within this framework that the many positions can be heard, the roles and polarities can form, and the issues present can be wrestled with. The dynamics found in large group interactions often reflect world situations, and as such, provide the possibility for new insight into global conflict and disturbance. Many positions are present within the large group that, if voiced, expand the identity of the group and bring new awareness of its diverse experiences. Dialogue in groups within the school system may take the form of a gathering of students, parents, and teachers, or it may involve the whole system when also inviting in administrators, members of school boards, and so on. The more levels of the system represented, the more the scope of the dialogue is expanded. The larger community may also be included in the dialogue situation, when representatives of the whole city attend. Here is an example of a group process conducted between parents, teachers, and school administrators some years ago.

> I am in the position of facilitator at a discussion about the imminent closing down of an alternative school in a local school district. Present at this meeting are the vice-superintendent of schools, the principal of the school, representatives from the teaching body, a group of about 25 parents and myself. Concern has been expressed at gossip circulating throughout the school about the school being shut down and students being allocated to other schools in the district. Parents have requested a meeting to express their views and to hear from decision-makers what is being planned.
>
> Up to this time, this alternative school had been affiliated to a public school, both schools being run by the same principal. The parents of the children attending the alternative school had formed a strong parents' association and up until the time of these developments had participated in the overall running of the school, attempting to maintain close connection with the principal and teachers. They now felt angry and disgruntled about being left out of ongoing plans and concerned about the future of their children. The students, picking up on their parents' anger, were reported to be sullen and rebellious at school. The atmosphere in the room is tense.
>
> As parents begin to express their concerns, allegations are made that the principal had been sabotaging all efforts of the parents to increase the numbers of the alternative school membership and to strengthen its establishment. As a result many potential pupils had been denied a place in the school, and numbers were falling below the

accepted minimum required by the Superintendent of Schools. Parents are angry about being manipulated and feel betrayed. I encourage them to go further in expressing their feelings and then support the principal to respond. He begins by attempting to defend himself against the allegations, denying they are true.

His attempts fail though, as his tone of voice and general demeanour do not quite go along with his expressed position. Although verbally he is standing strongly in support of the alternative school, he repeatedly looks down, fumbles with his pen and generally appears nervous. I make a facilitative comment at this point. "It must be difficult to bring out your own views here when being confronted by such a strong group of parents. I support you to speak freely and honestly as this will help to take the dialogue further, clear the air, and clarify a path for the future of the school."

Being acknowledged in this way allows the principal to go further in expressing himself congruently. His voice drops and he looks shame-faced as he shares that he has never been particularly interested in alternative schooling, but had felt compelled to accept the position as principal as he did not want to endanger his career in the school system. He had convinced himself that he would be able to do the position justice, and in fact had put a lot of attention into doing his best. Lately however, his duties as principal of both schools have become overwhelming for him, and he has been neglecting the alternative school. In addition, he has been feeling pressured by higher levels of the education system that no longer wish to financially support the alternative program and are hoping to eventually close it down.

The genuineness of the principal's sharing diffuses the escalating anger of the parents present who now turn to the vice-superintendent of schools for an explanation. They repeatedly challenge her for being unsupportive to the cause of the alternative school. In defense the vice-superintendent refers many times to the "education sector at government levels" as stipulating minimum numbers and as refusing to provide the necessary support to keep the school open. As parents talk about their disappointment at losing the kind of education for their children that they found so meaningful, the vice-superintendent begins to speak very personally about how establishing this school has also been a dream for her and about how much she is grieving the potential loss. She feels powerless against the decision of the higher education body.

> *The atmosphere in the room has now completely changed. People have drawn their chairs closer in to each other and are talking about their sadness and disappointment at losing the school. They decide to make contact with policy makers at government level (the missing role in this meeting) to try to avert the loss by stimulating change at higher levels of the system. The principal, vice-superintendent, teachers, and parents have formed a united group to take matters further.*

Having an opportunity to enter a facilitated dialogue over a contentious issue provided a container in which underlying views, positions, and feelings could be expressed and received. In unravelling presenting situations and going deeper into the personal experiences of those present, connection was made on a feeling level and the experiences of others were better understood. This opportunity contributed to an expansion of the group identity. The above group transformed its experience from a divided group experiencing relative disempowerment into a bonded group focused on becoming socially active in order to expand systemic awareness around the issue of alternative schooling.

Growth of awareness

An issue can be processed in a group dialogue at a particular time, and then this process may continue in other group situations when the same issue comes up again. Having encountered a dynamic in a group situation, awareness is also raised for individuals who may then continue to process the issue on an inner level or with others not as familiar with the situation. Roles, both represented and missing, being inherent parts of the issue in focus, might re-appear and be represented on an inner level, in relationship interactions, or in further group encounters on the same or similar issues. This helps to unfold the issue further. The growth of awareness and new insight reached in one group interaction, is but a step in an ongoing process of unfolding deeper and deeper layers of the issue addressed. Growth of new insight is therefore an ongoing process itself. One may reach a moment in a relationship or group encounter when the atmosphere changes and a new feeling component enters the room. When awareness of this shift is noticed and commented on by the facilitator, members of the group will often experience an individual change in attitude that can then also be integrated by the group. This may be seen as a moment of resolution. When the same issue is next encountered or processed, a deeper level is accessed due to the integration of the previous change in awareness. When these moments are encountered more frequently as a result of a group or individual working on issues in an ongoing way, change begins to be integrated on a long-term systemic basis and a sense of sustainable community begins to develop.

Resolution to a problem is not seen to be an end result that reflects the completion of a contentious issue. It is a moment when there is a shift in the feeling experiences of all present when some sort of understanding is gained. The *dreaming* of the group manifests the group's *true* identity, which is then held by the group experience and awareness. The known identity of the group is enlarged and new awareness cultivated. It is in this way that shadow material is embraced and transformed. For example, when a student complains of being controlled in the school situation and expresses her sense of being oppressed, the role of the oppressor can be represented in the group and can be expressed by one or more teachers who are willing to stand for the adherence to strict rules. These two parts then are able to dialogue with each other with the help of the facilitator, who encourages each side or role held to go deeper into its points of view and emotional reactions. In deepening expression of both of these, enhanced understanding of what lies beneath the surface behaviour is cultivated. When these parts next encounter each other, either in the classroom or in another group situation, awareness has already been expanded around this polarization, and change can be integrated into the relationship. When processed further in another dialogue, the process can unfold further bringing forth even more deeply imbedded unshared experience. This enriches the whole field adding to systemic understanding of the issue in question and leading to enhanced acceptance of previously marginalized individuals who have held unacceptable positions in the system. The issue of oppression, as in the above example, would therefore begin to be understood from a different perspective, allowing more leeway for diverse experiences of it on both sides of the issue.

Community

Mindell (1995) maintains that the sacred thing behind presenting chaos is community, the deepest idea of which is to be free and included. Community does not mean only peace, but also difference, dialogue, and discussion. One cannot get away from the conflict or disturbance. It has to be dealt with. In the dealing of it, relationships are deepened and a sense of community begins to form. "It's the feelings! That's what brings people together—when they feel something together. It's not only happiness that brings people together; it's the shared pain we have as human beings" (1994, p. 83). The real common ground is the emotions people share. We cannot accomplish the development of community without being able to embrace and work on emotional problems and differences underlying the tensions.

Scott Peck defines community as "a group of individuals who have learned how to communicate honestly with each other, whose relationships go deeper than their masks of composure and who have developed some significant commitment to rejoice together, mourn together and to delight in each other and make others' conditions their own" (1987, p. 59). He maintains that the necessary key is the appreciation of differences and the ability to be able to see the suffering and deeper components of our fellow human beings. He talks about how the ability to be wounded by the wounds of others creates a sense of sharing and community. The understanding that something is shared between people creates communion. Peck also maintains that when a community is created as a safe place, it can contain and support difference. If we can be together in community then we can begin to bring out our conflicts by communicating about them. Like Mindell, Peck maintains that chaos is an essential part of the community-making process, in which individual differences are brought out into the open to be negotiated, even though sometimes painfully, through adversity and confrontation. The bridge between chaos and community is discovered in those moments when conflicting positions are deepened to reveal the personal stories and views of individuals who begin to share their own visions, hopes, joys, brokenness, defeats, fears, failures, and pains. It is at this point, that each member can begin to understand others on the basis of this sharing as it touches something deep within them too.

Paulo Freire believes that every human being, no matter how silenced he may be, is "capable of looking critically at his world in a dialogical encounter with others" (Freire, 1988, p. 13). Given the right tools with which to dialogue, the perceptions of personal and social reality, including contradictions, can be perceived and dealt with critically. This ability to "name the world in our own way" empowers us and develops new dignity and hope. This is the practice of freedom by which we learn to deal creatively with reality and participate in the transformation of our world. Freire sees dialogue as an existential necessity. It is in speaking out and naming each individual's truth, that transformation of the world becomes possible. It is in this way that we achieve significance for our lives. He sees dialogue as an act of creation, which cannot exist without a profound love for the world and humanity. "Love is at the same time the foundation of dialogue and dialogue itself, and is a commitment to others and the cause of liberation" (p. 301).

Behind every area of tension and conflict, behind every group and group identity is a dream, vision, or myth trying to be lived, the consciousness and meaning of which emerges as the group engages and processes its issues. Community building relies on the ability of the group, with the help of the facilitator, to contact the background dreaming process that appears as something new trying to emerge in the group. New awareness often tries to make itself known through disturbance, conflict, relationship problems, and world issues. To be able to sit with these tensions in order to explore them provides a milieu in which the larger dreaming process can emerge. Mindell's idea is to make conflict and disturbance more useful, to see them as something rich and interesting in which to be engaged. Instead of endless disruption, he would like to see a process of change and transformation, a "dreaming together" towards a new community (Mindell, 1993). The idea of consciousness dreaming itself into existence through all of the experiences, interactions, signals, and events that occur is a concept discussed by Jung (1934), and other Jungian therapists (Edinger, 1992). Both the Bushpeople of Southern Africa and the Aboriginal people of Australia emphasize the importance of the development of group consciousness through the opportunity for group dialogue. They incorporate dialogue into their lives on a daily basis.

The opportunity to express and share visions, feelings, views, and personal experiences within the context of group situations is vital for the healthy continuance of group life and for the system in which groups abide. Through an appreciation of all forms of life and its diversity, we can develop the ability to support and understand others as well as ourselves. Modern theorists see difference as a gateway to the development of community, resting on the capacity to build bridges between those who may hold diverse views and positions. One way of doing this is through providing an environment and a model that promotes and supports discussion and dialogue among group members on both intra-group and inter-group levels. "Talk has the power to make the *I* of private self-interest into a *we* that makes possible civility and common political action" (Barber, 1984, p. 189). Talk nourishes empathy, and empathy develops bonds and promotes public thinking. The creation of community rests upon the recognition of how important all the parts are within a system. The creation of community also rests on an appreciation of how all parts contribute in an egalitarian way to the functioning of that system. Opportunities for the parts to interact and learn about each others' experiences, and to confront each other in conflicting or disturbing situations, enhances the sense of connectedness and commonness among them. It is when individuals are pained themselves about the pain that others have experienced, that bonds are formed and a safe place is created in which community can flourish.

CHAPTER SEVEN

Conclusion and final reflections

Socio-political and cultural dynamics

The Pink Floyd song *"Another Brick in the Wall"*, (Pink Floyd, 1979) reflects the victimization that students may feel at the hands of teachers. It also expresses the sense of abandonment felt when adults who are looked to for guidance and support, either attempt to control and dominate the kids, or leave them bereft of emotional support or understanding. The sense by those in control that the "evil" nature of kids will take over, is suffered by the students, who may begin to feel more and more isolated and misunderstood. From a socio-political perspective, a society that primarily identifies with valuing and loving children, tends to deny the resentment and dislike it may feel toward its children and adolescents. Violent feelings towards youth, while being consciously denied, are made obvious in the alarming numbers of young people who are incarcerated at the hands of a legal system mostly hostile to youth, and in the statistics showing the many incidents of child abuse.

Within the school system children can be seen as burdensome nuisances who are non-compliant, defying what is expected of them. An unconscious attitude permeating relationships between many teachers and students puts the child or adolescent in the role of the rebel who is expected to consciously go against the structure, rules, and regulations governing the system. Cultural and historical views of children, which are generally mistrustful of children's motivation finding children onerous, influence these relationships and result in the student feeling alienated as he or she is met with an attitude mostly devoid of love and appreciation. In addition, the system does not include each individual child in choices made to create the structure in which the student finds herself immersed on a daily basis. This exacerbates an already established pattern of marginalization of children that exists in the culture as a whole. The result is that students, not finding a place in the school system where they can be celebrated for their individuality, become resentful and angry, attempting to draw attention to themselves by acting out or creating disturbance. The emphasis on high achievement and rewards for those who excel over their peers, creates a climate of failure and competitiveness, which further adds to the alienation and lack of appreciation felt by many. In the background of students' interactions with administrators, teachers, and other students exists a range of emotions, including unconscious longing, hostility, and vengefulness. The school system projects onto individual school children, especially those who are outside of expected standards of behaviour, the qualities that have been unconsciously marginalized by the system itself. These children are then seen as disturbing, representing the aggressive, potentially violent tendencies that have been repressed within the system and the culture. As there is no acknowledgement that there is no place for denied aspects of human nature on individual and systemic levels, exploring the shadow on a collective level is avoided through scapegoating of the individual student, who is then punished or cast out of the collective fold.

In societies where aggression and violence are generally shunned on both individual and collective levels, there is no place where these kinds of feelings can be openly aired and expressed other than in the arena of war where they are allowed. As archetypal forces demand expression, the built-up repressed or denied material eventually shows itself, usually through explosive or brutal means directed against oneself or others. In the school context these days, aggression and violence is dealt with harshly, even from an early age, and the child quickly learns to subdue any feeling expression that may cause negative consequences from teachers, principals, and others who hold positions of rank within the school system. Yet, through my experiences with the groups and individuals with whom I have worked, it becomes evident that merely the opportunity to talk about personal anger and tendencies toward aggression provides an outlet for strong feelings, thus relieving them and reducing the need to act out the aggression. Not only does the individual child feel acknowledged and met on a personal level, but also encounters others who have a similar experience. The rapport established between the students through the shared dialogue helps to create feelings of connection with others, dispelling the states of alienation and isolation previously experienced.

Containment

Through the introduction of dreams, dream images, active imagination, unfolding of body experiences, and sharing of mythical tales, creative expression of previously unshared inner emotional experiences related to aggressive or violent tendencies is elicited. In using these forms to draw forth denied shadow material, the usual resistance encountered in attempting to connect with adolescents, particularly with disavowed parts, is disarmed. A container is developed in which students feel free to divulge material usually considered taboo. Insight and understanding into the nature of unexpressed feelings and fantasies, provides a framework in which we can become more aware of the meaning they hold for each of us.

When emotional expressions and aggressive acts are provided a container in which to show themselves, positive results are noticed in behaviour changes of youth addressed in this fashion. From interviews conducted with youth (Garbarino and deLara, 2002) it was noticed how often containment was perceived as missing. Adolescents showed little trust in the ability or willingness of adults to do anything about bullying situations. There was also little awareness among adults of the necessity of talking with children about difficulties. When referred to school counsellors, bullying situations were not sufficiently dealt with. This was illustrated in the composite case example of Jennifer in chapter five, where the school counsellor was ineffective in addressing her bullying situation. Community support is also generally absent in cases of bullying and aggression in school.

In scapegoating children who act in aggressive or violent ways, the collective consciousness also becomes alienated from its own nature in refusing to acknowledge violent aspects of itself. The lack of a container able to hold the experiences of the child in a non-judgmental way, exacerbates both individual and collective isolation and clearly illustrates the inability to contain collective experiences judged as wrong. As in the composite case example of Julie who suffered in her isolation for many years only to finally explode in order to get the attention she needed, one can see how ostracism by her peers and other school members, mirrors the attempt to eradicate uncomfortable, painful, and disturbing experiences from the system.

The school child who encounters challenges within the school environment that he or she is unable to meet, will seek for understanding, support, and encouragement. When this is lacking the child's problems often become too heavy a burden for the child to continue carrying alone. Isolation and alienation increase, adding to this burden. At this point the child may generally become depressed, secretive, self-destructive, or begin to show signs of aggression towards others. Containment of the initial signs of distress would imply creating a context of understanding and support for the whole range of emotions that the child may be experiencing. In containing these, the individual child will feel related to in an empathic way. The container will also provide a way of drawing attention to previously unrecognized inner experiences, a means to explore them in a supportive way, and the useful integration of their meaning into those difficult situations confronting the child on a daily basis. Not only does the individual experience of the child need containment, but attention also needs to be given to dynamics which occur among his or her peers in social and class situations at school. Working with students in a group context has proved very valuable. Ongoing support of this kind alleviates alienation suffered on intrapsychic levels as well as within the social context.

Symptoms, image, and myth

A number of meaningful aspects found in situations of alienation and violence in the school setting have been illustrated through the use of image and myth. The use of image creates a gateway into the world of denied archetypal material allowing for its expression and containment. When encountering image a numinous experience often ensues allowing connection with a deeper sense of who one truly is. Derek, the enraged adolescent who became aggressive and threatening in a group setting (described in chapter three), was able to access an understanding of the motivation lying beneath his aggressive behaviour. This motivation was mirrored in the images that emerged through his violent music reflecting his desire for a better world where individuals could be treated more fairly and equally. As a result he was able to get in touch, not only with his own pain, but also with a much deeper part of his numinous self, inspiring him to manifest this "knightly" image of himself more consciously in the face of his challenging life situation. Bringing forth these previously unrecognized parts of himself, freed him from being unconsciously locked into a way of relating to himself and the world which did not serve him. One can see here how the use of image can lift one out of an ingrained way of being to discover new meaning in life. The juiciness that emerged for Maria from the image of her rounded form as an apple is also a good example of the use of image as a guide to aspects of the true self. Process-oriented and imaginal methods used to enhance awareness are extremely useful in working with disturbed individuals in pain over life circumstances and suffering from harmful situations encountered within the school system.

Not only can the use of image and myth be useful on an individual level, it also brings an understanding of where meaning can be found in disavowed or unwanted experiences on a collective level. In exploring myths such as *Mother Moon*, the psyche is freed to enliven those parts previously imprisoned out of collective fear. In understanding that evil as represented in the form of Lucifer is a source of illumination, light is shed on the darkened areas of psyche where secrets and the shunned are held prisoners. Behaviours associated with evil may be better engaged in order to find the areas to which they are attempting to call attention. This understanding would greatly benefit the whole school system, and indeed the larger social system, and allow for better containment of disturbing patterns through the knowledge that these are in fact gateways to the development of further awareness.

Meaning and purpose

A point that I have emphasized many times is how meaningful disturbance can be when explored in a way that reveals its deeper purpose. In summarily judging behaviours as "bad" and in attempting to get rid of them, the school system robs itself of an opportunity for development. Disturbers of a collective identity might be meaningful for the system in which they exist if the deeper meaning of a disturbance can be used to contribute to the resolution of systemic shortcomings and difficulties. In being willing to explore the symptomatic aspects of the system itself, the *identified patient* needs to be recognized as a signal that something is wrong on the systemic level. This will call for changes to be made on a collective level as well, rather than placing the responsibility on a handful of individuals. Being willing to explore an established identity can be a frightening and daunting task. Remaining ignorant, while projecting the troublesome factors onto an identified disturber, is far more comfortable and less threatening.

When disturbing tendencies, such as the hatred of others and the desire to kill are entertained and discussed, not only can impulses such as these be expressed, but the underlying emotional content of these phenomena can also be accessed. In allowing emotional expression, phenomena considered as "bad" can be brought to light and explored. Concomitant experiences of shame and anger are placated by a teleological approach that is able to embrace phenomena as natural and transformative. In exploring impulses to hurt and kill others, group members were not only relieved of these burdensome feelings, but were also able to increase their self-awareness, contacting strong aspects of themselves which they had not previously identified. When belief systems become too one-sided the unconscious is likely to constellate some challenge to that, manifesting something that creates disturbance. Archetypal energy that needs to emerge then shows itself in the disturbance, challenging one to attend to it. The symptom serves psychic equilibrium by emerging as a disruption. In this way it attempts to invite consciousness of itself. In the school system's emphasis on perfectionism and compliance, experiences that do not support these goals are marginalized. As many of the marginalized experiences are a part of human nature, a backlash occurs.

Experiences of alienation and related aggression, shame, and a desire for vengeance, become a reflection of the symptomatic one-sidedness of the system in its disregard of the shadow side of human nature. Developing an aptitude for dealing with the whole range of human experience would be a meaningful resolution when exploring symptomatic signs.

According to Machiavelli, a prince should not deviate from what is good if that is possible, but he should know how to do evil if that is necessary (Samuels, 1991). Machiavelli was able to make a morality out of the shadow content usually disowned. Stella, the schoolgirl mentioned who took out her penknife to ward off her attackers when no protection was available for her from school staff, is an embodiment of this principle. Her later satisfaction at having protected herself allowed her to embrace a side of herself which was frowned on within the school system, but which proved useful to her. This act later empowered her to make some very meaningful decisions for herself, as well as giving her a more rounded perspective of herself and her own power, adding to her sense of self-value and trust.

A new mythology of violence is created when no vessel is provided within the family or cultural context for the containment of disavowed emotions. This new mythology suggests that we can be masters over our aggression by learning to use it skilfully rather than destructively. In addressing perpetrators of bullying and school violence, positive results are obtained when a container is provided in which to explore the disturbing behaviours in order to extract something meaningful and useful from them. In this way a transformation occurs in which aggressive energy can be usefully channelled, thus fulfilling a meaningful function.

Alienation

Alienation of the self, in which the self is divested of its reality in favour of external roles or fantasies, can lead to a loss of connection with the true self. In an effort to fit the approved model, the individual may commit actions bringing him or her into disharmony with the self. The many emotional reactions experienced then, such as shame, hopelessness, anger, depression, and so on, further alienate the individual from self.

Teachers are also alienated from the students and school community, resulting in a lack of personal bonding. So many students pass through a teacher's class on a regular basis there is little opportunity for personal contact between teachers and students. Instead of dialoguing with students about infractions, imposition of punishments and harsher regulations are common events. Due to class size and pressure to complete syllabi, overworked teachers feel alienated themselves, unable to make the contact they would like with students and other teachers. Also associated with overcrowded classes, are students' experiences of being unrecognized on an individual basis. This adds to their sense of alienation within the system, particularly if they are also children who are excluded by their peer groups. Exacerbating this situation is the lack of support for intrapsychic development and appreciation for individual characteristics not associated with academic or athletic achievement. In addition, little focus or recognition is given to the imaginative life of children and their unique creativity, thus further alienating important aspects of themselves.

Particularly suffering from a sense of alienation are those youth who are considered to be the perpetrators of aggressive or violent acts. In many cases (Moore et al. 2003) it was found that these youth experienced alienation from adults in their communities, that parents had little ability to communicate with them, and that they were ostracized and condemned for their disturbing activities. Providing containment for the expression of difficulties associated with this pattern, alleviates many of the misunderstandings that arise from observing associated disturbing behaviours, allowing a context in which all members of the system could find support for expression of their experiences. The opportunity to dialogue and share personal experiences in a group context is extremely valuable in dispelling experiences of alienation and in fostering a sense of connection with others. I would recommend facilitated group encounters and open group discussions among students, teachers, parents, and the whole school membership on an ongoing basis as a remedial method in addressing systemic problems.

The disturber's psychological dynamics

Although individual acts of violence are seen as destructive they are also a cry of hope; hope for inclusion, recognition and acknowledgement; hope that someone will break through the wall of isolation;

hope that the pain will come to an end. Hope, and actions that derive from it, provide an attempt to be creative in an impossible situation. Caught in a quagmire that torments and consumes him, the individual reaches out in a disturbing way from a place of desperation. Violence leads to contact with others, breaking through the alienation surrounding the imprisoned self.

The following dynamics are shown to exist for children and adolescents who express through aggressive and violent acts.

- Both intrapsychic and interpersonal shaming are related to the strong emphasis on achievement and perfection found in schools. Shame, self-blame, and self-hatred are linked to the alienation of psychic retreat when failing to fulfil expectations or to receive recognition for efforts made.
- Self-hatred grows rapidly when the child is faced with exclusion from peer groups, bullying, and personal lack of acknowledgement. Social standing in school and among peers is of utmost concern to most youth and exclusion, teasing, and bullying detrimentally effect self-esteem, self-image, and self-value.
- A grandiose self is created to offset internal inadequacy experienced. Fearing to wield any power at all, grandiosity falsely engenders a sense of power and control. Internal grandiose beliefs relieve the fear and humiliation of feeling powerless. Grandiosity may also lead to impulsive and inflated acts.
- Rage, hatred, and envy are strongly felt when the individual is excluded, ridiculed, or overlooked. When there is no change in the outer situation, pent-up and repressed destructive impulses may burst out, providing retribution for the pain suffered. Acts of revenge temporarily bring a sense of restitution while momentarily empowering the aggressor.
- Violent acts may also reflect an unconscious longing for recognition, contact, and belonging. Physical and emotional violence provide a way of connecting with others when relationship has been withheld or denied.

The relationship between alienation and violence

The more youth experience being alienated from the system, the more self-alienation evolves. Often self-alienation leads to also alienating others from oneself, inculcating a pervasive emptiness longing to be filled. When socially approved attempts to break through the bubble of alienation fail, the individual may resort to desperate acts of violence. The alienated self then calls out for help through acts of aggression and hatred. Self-hatred and self-blame engender destructive forces aimed toward the self. The self, in order to survive in some fashion, is forced to hide from these resulting in isolation and estrangement from the true self. Associated with strong negative reactions towards oneself, and thus alienation of the true self, are hateful and vengeful impulses toward others who are perceived as owning the very recognition and inclusion longed for by the alienated one.

Jungian, mythical, and psychodynamic views all point to the relationship between alienation and violence. In Jungian psychology the figures that embody these qualities can be seen in collective symbolism and dream figures. Archetypal forces are expressed in the fury at not being heard and the engagement in vengeful and terrorizing acts in order to gain acknowledgement. Many fairy tales and myths depict the character who is cast out of the community, only to return with vengeance in his heart seeking retribution for the great hurt received. Satan himself is a representative of this image. Falling from grace, he becomes imbued with evil, representing the shadow aspect of all that is good. So too, the child or adolescent perceived as "failing", not fitting in with peers, and ostracized by the system, becomes filled with self-doubt, shame, and hatred, suffering the pain of alienation. Ensuing psychodynamic factors leading to greater alienation and pain may at last be relieved by a reckless outburst of fury and violence, temporarily restoring an experience of being "real". In this way, reparation is claimed and a moment of peace discovered. The experience is one of redeeming the self.

The next steps

The main focus of this book has been the aggressive and violent behaviours found within the school system. Emphasis has been placed on the influences within the school context on students, and in particular on students who may be prone to behaviour disturbances. Applying the insights gained through this focus would generally call for a change in school structure, necessitating more training of school teachers and counsellors, hands-on interventions over the long-term with children and adolescents expressing difficulties in the social fabric at school, increased democratic focus providing more choiceful alternatives for school students and teachers, and more opportunities for group dialogue and processing between all parts of the system including students, parents, teachers, principals, administrators, school boards, and so on. This would certainly call for greater and improved funding of educational endeavours. The majority of research on violence is based on a multi-factor approach. According to this approach, effective intervention and prevention should also assess the teacher's work, take into account the structure of the school, and reflect the educational approach practiced at a particular school. The entire school needs to be the focus and not only the behaviour of the students (Balser, Schrewe & Wegricht, 2005).

More research is needed in finding ways to address and replace a perfectionist/achievement-oriented system with one that is more conducive to appreciation of the uniqueness of each individual child, where the quality of the attempt rather than the achievement could be acknowledged. How to provide containment for difficult emotions, how to empower individual students and address family concerns, how to replace control with personal responsibility, and above all how to support dialogue, are important areas for further study. Such topics as improved teaching methods, more interesting curricula, more congenial environments, and opportunities for artistic expressions, are all part of the extensive research and implementation that needs to be carried out in order to fully address shortcomings in the school system as a whole. These areas of further study and practical application are but a few among the many areas that could be addressed. What is important is that research and study in this arena be not only theoretically oriented, but practically implemented in as many ways as possible. Immediate and practical ways are urgently needed to address the ever-increasing alienation and violence found within schools worldwide. In order to avert more disasters such as those being encountered repeatedly, immediate engagement at all levels of the school system is a necessity.

Another huge field that connects in with that of school violence is the family environment and the many influences on disturbed youth held in inter-generational and family patterns. This field covers issues of abuse, neglect, poverty, race, psychiatry, and many other factors not touched on here. Much more needs to be explored in these areas in terms of their affect on expressions of school violence and how preventive measures could be developed. This would call for extensive funding and the creation of infrastructures to address and support family dis-ease and its rehabilitation.

Rollo May offers a reminder that, "for the self-respecting human being, violence is always an ultimate possibility, resorted to less if admitted than if suppressed" (Diamond 1996, p. 28). It is when existence becomes unendurable that the individual may exercise the inalienable human right to take one's own life or another's. Alienation and isolation contribute to making life unbearable when unable to find solace, love, support, or intimacy. The process of increasing rage is described as follows:

> Violence is the ultimate destructive substitute which surges in to
> fill the vacuum where there is no related-ness .... When inward
> life dries up, when feeling decreases and apathy increases,
> when one cannot affect or even genuinely *touch* another person,
> violence flares up as a daimonic necessity for contact, a mad
> drive, forcing touch in the most direct way possible.

In a social milieu rapidly moving toward a state of almost total alienation everything becomes transformed into a commodity. "Not only things, but the person himself, his physical energy, his skills, his knowledge, his opinions, his feelings, even his smiles" (Fromm, 1973, p. 388). Mirroring the social view of oneself as a commodity, one loses touch with what it means to be a human being, rich in feelings, imagination, creativity, and connectedness. The pain of this loss, although repressed and unconscious, must become evident in some way. Violent acts provide this means, breaking through the impenetrable numbness.

In emphasizing other ways in which the walls of disapproval and denial may be breached before aggressive or violent acts burst through, I have emphasized the importance of reaching in to touch children and adolescents in their places of most vulnerability. In opening a space in which hated feelings can be acknowledged and understood, in which pain and hurt can be divulged, rejected personal experiences are invited to step through the wall of repression to reveal their nature and potential. A blush of red is restored to youthful cheeks as the youth behind the mask comes alive. The withdrawn and hateful teen can be transformed into a vital, expressive character, jumping into life with a full-lipped smile on a glowing face. What it takes is a little time to reach out, to look, and to listen.

BIBLIOGRAPHY

ABC News Channel. (1999) http://more.abcnews.go.com/sections/ us/DailyNews/schoolshootings990420.html990621

Abecassis, M. (1999). I Dislike You and You Dislike Me: Prevalence and Developmental Significance of Mutual Antipathies among Pre-adolescents and Adolescents. (Unpublished doctoral dissertation, University of Minnesota).

Abecassis, M. (2003). I Hate You Just the Way You Are: Exploring the Formation, Maintenance and Need for Enemies. *New Directions for Child and Adolescent Development, 102*: 5–22.

Adler, A. (1929). *The Practice and Theory of Individual Psychology.* London: Kegan Paul, Trench, Trubner.

Akhtar, S. Kramer, S. & Parens, H. (1995). *The Birth of Hatred: Developmental, Clinical and Technical Aspects of Intense Aggression.* New Jersey: Jason Aronson Inc.

Anderson, M. (2007). *Dialogue in Uncertainty.* Public Lecture, Oregon Psychoanalytic Center.

Arendt, H. (1970). *On Violence.* New York: Harcourt, Brace.

Ayers, M. (2000). The Eyes of Shame. (Doctoral dissertation, Pacifica Graudate Institute, 2000). Proquest Dissertations And Theses. UMI no. 3081676.

Balser, H. Schrewe, H. & Wegricht, R. (Eds.). (2005). Regionale Gewaltpravention Strategien und Erfahrungen. In: A. Guggenbuhl, K. Hersberger, T. Rom & P. Bostrom (Eds.), *Helping Schools in Crisis* (p. 3). City: IKM Guggenbuhl AG.

Barber, J.D. (1984). *Citizen Politics*. Chicago: Markham Publishing.

Bell-Fialkoff, A. (1999). *Ethnic Cleansing*. New York: St. Martin's Griffin.

Bell, C.L. (2004). The Contribution of Narcissism and Peer Rejection to the Psychological Internalization Process of the Classroom Avenger. *Dissertation Abstracts International: Section B: The Sciences and Engineering, 64*(10-B): p. 5206.

Berry, P. (1982). *Echo's Subtle Body*. Woodstock, CT: Spring.

Bettelheim, B. (1975). *The Uses of Enchantment: The Meaning and Importance of Fairy Tales*. New York: Penguin Books.

Bion, W. (1957). The Differentiation of the Psychotic from the Non-Psychotic Part of the Personality. *International Journal of Psychoanalysis, 38*: 266–75.

Blum, H.P. (1995). Sanctified Aggression, Hate and the Alteration of Standards. In: S. Akhtar, S. Kramer & H. Parens (Eds.), *The Birth of Hatred: Developmental, Clinical and Technical Aspects of Intense Aggression* (pp. 15–39). New Jersey: Aronson.

Bohm, D. (1980). *Wholeness and the Implicate Order*. London: Routledge and Kegan Paul.

Columbine High School Massacre (2006, October 28). In *Wikipedia, The free encyclopedia*. Retrieved October 18, 2006, from http://en.wikipedia.org/wiki

Conant, J.B. (1959). *The American High School Today: A First Report for Interested Citizens*. New York: McGraw Hill.

Corbett, L. (1996). *The Religious Function of the Psyche*. London: Routledge.

Corbin, H. (1972). *Mundus Imaginalis or the Imaginary and the Imaginal*. Spring.

Dale, F.M.J. (1993). Unconscious Communication of Hatred Between Parents and Children. In: Varma, V. (Ed.), *How and Why Children Hate: A Study of Conscious and Unconscious Sources* (pp. 17–30). Philadelphia: Jessica Kingsley.

de Mare, P.G., Piper, R. & Thompson, S. (1991). *Koinonia. From Hate through Dialogue to Culture in the Large Group*. London: Karnac Books.

deMause, L. (2002). *The Emotional Life of Nations*. New York: Other Press.

Dewey, J. (1916). *Democracy and Education*. New York: Free Press.

Diamond, S.A. (1996). *Anger, Madness, and The Daimonic: The Psychological Genesis of Violence, Evil and Creativity*. Albany, NY: State University of New York Press.

Dodge, K.A. (1983). Behavioral Antecedents of Peer Social Status. *Child Development*, 54: 1386–1399.

Dodge, K.A. & Coie, J.D. (1987). Social-Information-Processing Factors in Reactive and Proactive Aggression in Children's Peer Groups. *Journal of Personality and Social Psychology*, 53(6): 1146–1158.

Dwivedi, K.N. (1993). Child Abuse and Hatred. In: Varma, V. (Ed.), *How and Why Children Hate: A Study of Conscious and Unconscious Sources* (pp. 46–71). Philadelphia: Jessica Kingsley.

Eckert, P. (1989). *Jocks and burnouts: Social Categories and Identity in the High School*. New York: Teachers College Press.

Edinger, E.F. (1984). *The Creation of Consciousness*. Toronto, Canada: Inner City Books.

Edinger, E.G. (1992). *Transformation of the God-image*. Toronto, Canada: Inner City Books.

Envy (2002). In: J. Pearsall and B. Trumble (Eds.), *The Oxford English Reference Dictionary*. New York: Oxford University Press.

Fallis, K.R. & Opotow, S. (2003). Are Students Failing in School or are Schools Failing Students? *Journal of Social Issues*, 59(1): 103–119.

Frankl, V. (1984). *Man's Search for Meaning*. NJ: Washington Square Press.

Freire, P. (1988). *Pedagogy of the Oppressed*. New York: Continuum.

Freud, S. (1995). Instincts and their Vicissitudes. *Standard Edition 14*: 109–140. In: Akhtar, S. Kramer, S. & Parens, H. (1995). *The Birth of Hatred: Developmental, Clinical and Technical Aspects of Intense Aggression*. New Jersey: Jason Aronson Inc. (Original work published 1916).

Fildes, V. (1986). *Breasts, Bottles and Babies*. Edinburgh: Edinburgh University Press.

Follett, M.P. (1965). *The New State: Group Organization the Solution of Popular Government*. Gloucester, MA: Peter Smith.

Fromm, E. (1973). *The Anatomy of Human Destructiveness*. New York: Henry Holt and Company.

Frude, N. (1993). Hatred Between Children. In: Varma, V. (Ed.), *How and Why Children Hate: A Study of Conscious and Unconscious Sources* (pp. 72–93). Philadelphia: Jessica Kingsley.

Garbarino, J. & deLara, E. (2002). *And Words Can Hurt Forever. How to Protect Adolescents from Bullying, Harassment, and Emotional Violence.* New York: Free Press.

Garrett, A.G. (2003). *Bullying in American Schools: Causes, Preventions and Interventions.* Jefferson, NC: McFarland.

Gay, P. (Ed.). (1989). *The Freud Reader.* New York: Norton.

Giegerich, W. (2001). *The Soul's Logical Life.* Frankfurt: Peter Lang.

Goldstein, A.P., Palumbo, J., Striepling, S. & Voutsinas, A.M. (1995). *Break it Up: A Teacher's Guide to Managing Student Aggression.* Champaign, IL: Research Press.

Goth (2006, October 18). In *Wikipedia, The Free Encyclopedia.* Retrieved October 18, 2006, from http://en.wikipedia.org/wiki/Goth

Gottfredson, G.D. & Gottfredson, D.C. (1985). *Victimization in Schools.* New York: Plenum Press.

Grotstein, J. (2007). *The Voice from the Crypt: The Negative Therapeutic Reaction and the Longing for a Childhood that Never Was.* Public Lecture, Oregon Psychoanalytic Center.

Guggenbuhl, A. (1997). *The Incredible Fascination of Violence.* Woodstock, CT: Spring.

Guggenbuhl, A. (1998). *Mythodrama.* Zurich: IKM Guggenbuhl AG.

Guggenbuhl, A., Hersberger, K., Rom, T. & Bostrom, P. (2000). *Helping Schools in Crisis: A Scientific Evaluation of the Mythodramatic Intervention Approach in Swiss and Swedish Schools.* Zurich: IKM Guggenbuhl AG.

Guggenbuhl-Craig, A. (1990). Why Psychopaths Do Not Rule the World. In: C. Zweig & J. Abrams. *Meeting the Shadow: The Hidden Power of the Dark Side of Human Nature* (pp. 223–226). New York: Tarcher/Putnam.

Gutmann, A. (1999). *Democratic Education.* Princeton, NJ: Princeton University Press.

Haller, E.J. (1992, Summer). High School Size And Student Indiscipline: Another Aspect Of the School Consolidation Issue? *Educational Evaluation and Policy Analysis, 14*: 145–156.

Hamburg, D.A. (1963). *Expression of the Emotions in Man.* New York: International Universities Press.

Hamilton, J. & Cairns, R. (eds.) (1961). *The Collected Dialogues of Plato.* New York: Pantheon.

Hannah, B. (1981). *Encounters with the Soul: Active Imagination as Developed by C.G. Jung.* Santa Monica, CA: Sigo Press.

Hedges, C. (2002). *War is a Force that Gives us Meaning.* New York: Anchor Books.

Hermeneuin (2002). In: J. Pearsall and B. Trumble (Eds.), *The Oxford English Reference Dictionary.* New York: Oxford University press.

Hillman, J. (1975), *Revisioning Psychology.* New York: Harper Perennial

Hillman, J. (1983). *Healing Fiction.* Putnam, CT: Spring.

Hillman, J. (2004). *A Terrible Love of War.* New York: Penguin

Hodges, E.V.E. & Card, N.A. (2003) *Enemies and the Darker Side of Peer Relations.* San Francisco: Jossey-Bass.

Homer (1968). *The Odyssey of Homer* (R. Lattimore, Trans.). New York: Harper & Row.

Hull, J.W. (2003). The Wilderness of Belonging: A Study of the Transformative Power of Intentional Community. (Doctoral dissertation, Pacifica Graduate Institute, 2003). Proquest Information and Learning Company. UMI no. 3155816.

Johnson, R.A. (1986). *Inner Work: Using Dreams and Active Imagination for Personal Growth.* San Francisco: Harper & Row.

Jung, C.G. (1953). Two Essays on Analytical Psychology. In: H. Read, M. Fordham, G. Adler, and W. McGuire (Eds.), *The Collected Works of C.G.Jung* (R.F.C. Hull, Trans.) (Vol. 7, p. 131). London: Routledge & Kegan Paul.

Jung, C.G. (1956). Symbols of Transformation. In: H. Read, M. Fordham, G. Adler, and W. McGuire (Eds.), *The Collected Works of C.G. Jung* (R.F.C. Hull, Trans.) (Vol. 5). London: Routledge & Kegan Paul.

Jung, C.G. (1959). Aion: Researches into the Phenomenology of the Self. In: H. Read, M. Fordham, G. Adler, and W. McGuire (Eds.), *The Collected Works of C.G. Jung* (R.F.C. Hull, Trans.) (Vol. 9, ii, p. 266). London: Routledge & Kegan Paul.

Jung, C.G. (1964). Civilization in Transition. In: H. Read, M. Fordham, G. Adler, and W. McGuire (Eds.), *The Collected Works of C.G. Jung* (R.F.C. Hull, Trans.) (Vol. 10). London: Routledge & Kegan Paul.

Jung, C.G. (1965). *Memories, Dreams, Reflections* (A. Jaffe, Ed.) (C. Winston & R. Winston, Trans.). New York: Vintage Books.

Jung, C.G. (1969). The Structure and Dynamics of the Psyche. In: H. Read, M. Fordham, G. Adler, and W. McGuire (Eds.), *The Collected Works of C.G. Jung* (R.F.C. Hull, Trans.) (Vol. 8). London: Routledge & Kegan Paul.

Jung, C.G. (1974). Dreams. (R.F.C. Hul, Trans.). Princeton, NJ: Princeton University Press.

Kaplan Williams, S. (1977). *The Art of Jungian-Senoi Dreamwork*. Berkeley, CA: Journey Press.

Katch, J. (2001). *Under Deadman's Skin: Discovering the Meaning of Children's Violent Play*. Boston: Beacon Press.

Kaufman, G. (1992). *Shame: The Power of Caring*. Rochester, VT: Shenkman Books.

Kernberg, O. (1992). *Aggression in Personality Disorders and Perversions*. New Haven: Yale University Press.

Kernberg, O. (1995). Hatred as a Core Affect of Aggression. In: S. Akhtar, S. Kramer & H. Parens (Eds.), *The birth of hatred: Developmental, Clinical and Technical Aspects of Intense Aggression*. New Jersey: Aronson.

Klein, M. (1988). *Envy and Gratitude and other Works 1946–1963*. London: Virago Press.

Kristeva, J. (1991). *Strangers to Ourselves*. Roudiez L.S. (Trans.). New York: Columbia University Press.

Lerner, M. (2000). *Spirit Matters*. Charlottesville, VA: Hampton Roads.

Limber, S.P. & Small, M.A. (2003). State Laws and Policies to Address Bullying in Schools. *School Psychology Review, 32*(3): 445.

McGee, J.P. & DeBernardo, C.R. (1999). The Classroom Avenger: A Behavioral Profile of School Based Shootings. *The Forensic Examiner, 8*(5): 16–18.

Martin, J.R. (2005). Becoming Educated: A Journey of Alienation or Integration? In: H.S. Shapiro & D.E. Purpel (Eds.), *Critical Social Issues in American Education: Democracy and Meaning in a Globalizing World*. New Jersey: Erlbaum.

Mathabane, M. (1987). *Kaffir Boy*. New York: Macmillan.

Meloy, J.R. (1988). *The Psychopathic Mind: Origins, Dynamics, and Treatment*. New Jersey: Jason Aronson.

Meloy, J.R., Hempel, A.G., Mohandie, K., Shiva, A.A. & Gray, B.T. (2001). Offender and Offense Characteristics of a Nonrandom Sample of Adolescent Mass Murders. *Journal of the American Academy of Child and Adolescent Psychiatry, 40*(6): 719–728.

Mindell, A. (1985). *River's Way*. New York: Routledge.

Mindell, A. (1988). *City Shadows: Psychological Interventions in Psychiatry*. New York: Routledge.

Mindell, A. (1992). *The Leader as Martial Artist: An Introduction to Deep Democracy*. San Francisco: Harper.

Mindell, A. (1993). Sitting in the Fire. Unpublished manuscript.

Mindell, A. (1995). *Sitting in the Fire: Large Group Transformation using Conflict and Diversity.* Portland, OR: Lao Tse Press.

Mindell, A. (2000). *Quantum Mind: The Edge between Physics and Psychology,* Portland, OR: Lao Tse Press.

Moore, R.L. (1989). *The Psychology of Satan: Encountering the Dark Side of the Self.* (Cassette Recording). Evanston, IL: C. G. Jung Institute of Chicago.

Moore, M.H., Petrie, C., Braga, A., and McLaughlin, B.L. (eds.) (2003). *Deadly Lessons: Understanding Lethal School Violence.* Washington, DC: The National Academies Press.

Morrell, R. (2002, February). A Calm after the Storm? Beyond Schooling as Violence. *Educational Review* 54(1): 37–46.

Morrison, A. (1989). *The Underside of Narcissism.* London: Analytic Press.

National Center for Education Statistics. (1997). *Violence and Discipline Problems in U.S. Public Schools: 1996–97.* Washington, DC: U.S. Department of Education.

National Center for Education Statistics. (2000). *Violence in U.S. Public Schools: School Survey on Crime and Safety.* Washington, DC: U.S. Department of Education.

Ninck (1936). *Wotan und germanische Schicksalsglaube.* In: C.G. Jung (1964). Civilization in Transition. In: H. Read, M. Fordham, G. Adler, and W. McGuire (Eds.), *The Collected Works of C.G. Jung* (R.F.C. Hull, Trans.) London: Routledge & Kegan Paul, 1946).

Olweus, D. (1993). *Bullying at School: What we Know and What we Can Do.* Malden, MA: Blackwell.

PBS (1998). www.pbs.org/wgbh/pages/frontline/shows/kinkel/etc/confesst.html

Pardeck, J.T. (2001). Children's Rights and School Violence. *International Journal of Adolescence and Youth,* 10(1–2): 147–155.

Pearsall, J. & Trumble, B. (Eds.). (2002). *Oxford English Reference Dictionary.* Second edition revised. Oxford University press.

Peck, S. (1987). *The Different Drum: Community Making and Peace.* New York: Simon and Schuster.

Perera, S.B. (1986). *The Scapegoat Complex: Toward a Mythology of Shadow and Guilt.* Toronto: Inner City Books.

Piers, M. (1978). *Infanticide.* New York: Norton.

Pink Floyd (1979). *The Wall.* USA: Capitol Records.

Pinkola-Estes, C. (1990). *Warming the Stone Child* (CD Recording No. 104D). Boulder, CO: Sounds True.

Purpel, D.E. (2000). Goals 2000: The Triumph of Vulgarity and the Legitimation of Social Injustice. In: H. S. Shapiro & D. E. Purpel (Eds.), *Critical Social Issues in American Education: Democracy and Meaning in a Globalizing World* (pp. 183–187). New Jersey: Erlbaum.

Rodkin, P.C., Pearl, R., Farmer, T.W. & van Acker, R. (2003). Enemies in the Gendered Societies of Middle Childhood: Prevalence, Stability, Associations with Social Status and Aggression. *New Directions for Child and Adolescent Development*, 102: 73–88.

Rohner, R.P. (1975). *They Love Me, They Love Me Not: A Worldwide Study of the Effects of Parental Acceptance and Rejection.* New Haven, CT: HRAF Press.

Rury, J.L. (2005). Democracy's High School? Social Change and American Secondary Education in the Post-Conant Era. In: H.S. Shapiro & D.E. Purpel (Eds.), *Critical Social Issues in American Education: Democracy and Meaning in A Globalizing World* (p. 57). New Jersey: Erlbaum.

Samuels, A. (1991). *The Mirror and the Hammer: Depth Psychology and Political Transformation* [Cassette Recording]. San Francisco, CA: C.G. Jung Institute of San Francisco.

Seita, R.J. & Brendtro, L.K. (2003). Adversarial Contests or Respectful Alliances. *Reclaiming Children and Youth*, 12(1): pp. 58–60.

Shapiro, S. (2005). Public School Reform: The Mismeasure of Education. In: H.S. Shapiro & D. E. Purpel (Eds.), *Critical Social Issues in American Education: Democracy and Meaning in a Globalizing World* (pp. 287–295). New Jersey: Erlbaum.

Society for the Advancement of Education. (1999, December). *Climate of Alienation can Trigger Violence. USA Today*, 128(2655): 12.

St. Clair, M. (2000). *Object Relations and Self Psychology.* Belmont, CA: Brooks/Cole.

Stein, M. (1995). *Jung on Evil.* Princeton, NJ: Princeton University Press.

Stein, M. (2006). *The Symbolic Life, Preparation and Practice.* Public Lecture, Friends of C.G. Jung, Portland, Oregon.

Storr, A. (1983). *The Essential Jung.* Princeton, NJ: Princeton University Press.

Summers, G. (1994). Conflict: Gateway to Community. Unpublished doctoral dissertation. The Union Institute.

Taffel, R. (1999). Discovering our Children: The Connection between Anonymity and Rage in Today's Kids. *Family Therapy Networker*, 23(5):

Weinstein, F. & Platt, G.M. (1973). *Psychoanalytic Sociology: An Essay on the Interpretation of Historical Data and the Phenomena of Collective Behavior*. Baltimore, MD: John Hopkins University Press.

Whitmont, E.C. (1990). The Evolution of the Shadow. In: C. Zweig & J. Abrams, *Meeting the Shadow: The Hidden Power of the Dark Side of Human Nature*. New York: Tarcher/Putnam.

Winnicott, D.W. (1976). *The Maturational Process and the Facilitating Environment*. London: The Hogarth Press.

Winnicott, D.W. (1984). *Deprivation and Delinquency*. London: Tavistock.

Wurmser, L. (1997). *The Mask of Shame*. Baltimore, MD: John Hopkins University Press.

INDEX

139